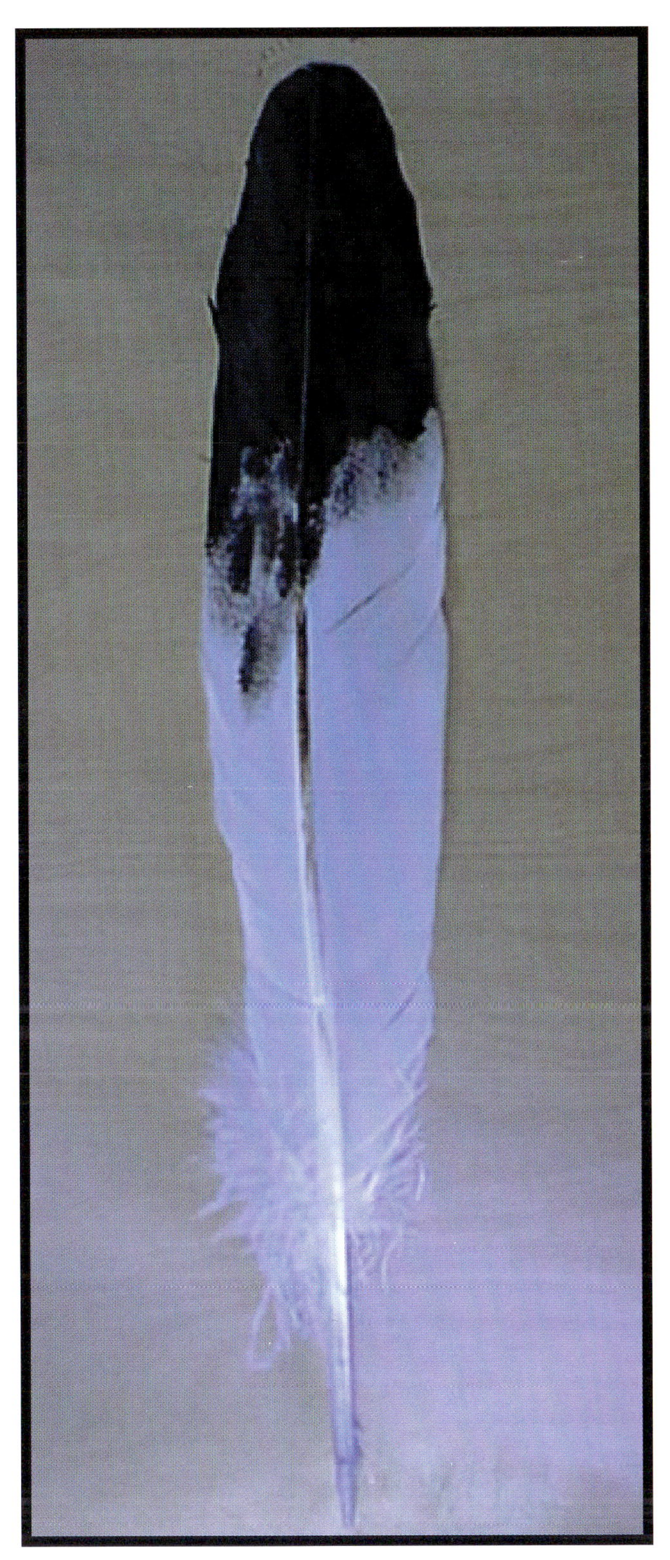

The Art of Simulating Eagle Feathers

by
Bob Gutierrez

Eagle's View Publishing
A WestWind, Inc. Company
6756 North Fork Road
Liberty, UT 84310

Library of Congress Number: 99-71332
ISBN: 0-943604-59-1

EAGLE'S VIEW FIRST EDITION

15 14 13 12 11 10 9 8 7 6 5 4 3 2 1

Introduction

In the early 1960s laws were passed to protect predatory and migratory birds, making the use and possession of their parts and feathers illegal.

In reproducing Native American artifacts the inability to use these items has resulted in the need for the production of a realistic substitute. This pamphlet focuses on the creation of a realistic substitute for the tail feathers of the immature Golden Eagle.

Since 1969, I've experimented with various types of feathers and pigments. I have used fabric dyes, leather dyes, oil wood stain, acrylics, markers, oil paint, hair dye, horn dye, hoof dye, taxidermist lacquer, inks, spray enamel, and spray latex.

I have found that although many of these mediums provide adequate color, some do not. Some provide adequate color but are not color fast, resulting in smearing and spotting.

The effect of medium on the feather is also a consideration. Some materials color well but do not penetrate the feather fiber, some will not color well enough, some damage the feather (*i.e.* make them brittle, "burn" the web etc.).

Turkey wing feathers are my feather of choice, not only because they are fairly large and make a good imitation, but they are also readily available, legal and affordable.

If the directions in this booklet are followed you can produce a number of simulated eagle feathers that will look quite real. We will start with an immature Golden Eagle tail feather.

Before you begin

It should be noted that the only way to build realistic feathers is to know what a good feather looks like. I have found that the study of photographs and the actual species, if possible, is a good way to start; however, one of the best means of studying individual feathers is to photocopy one and use it as a model.

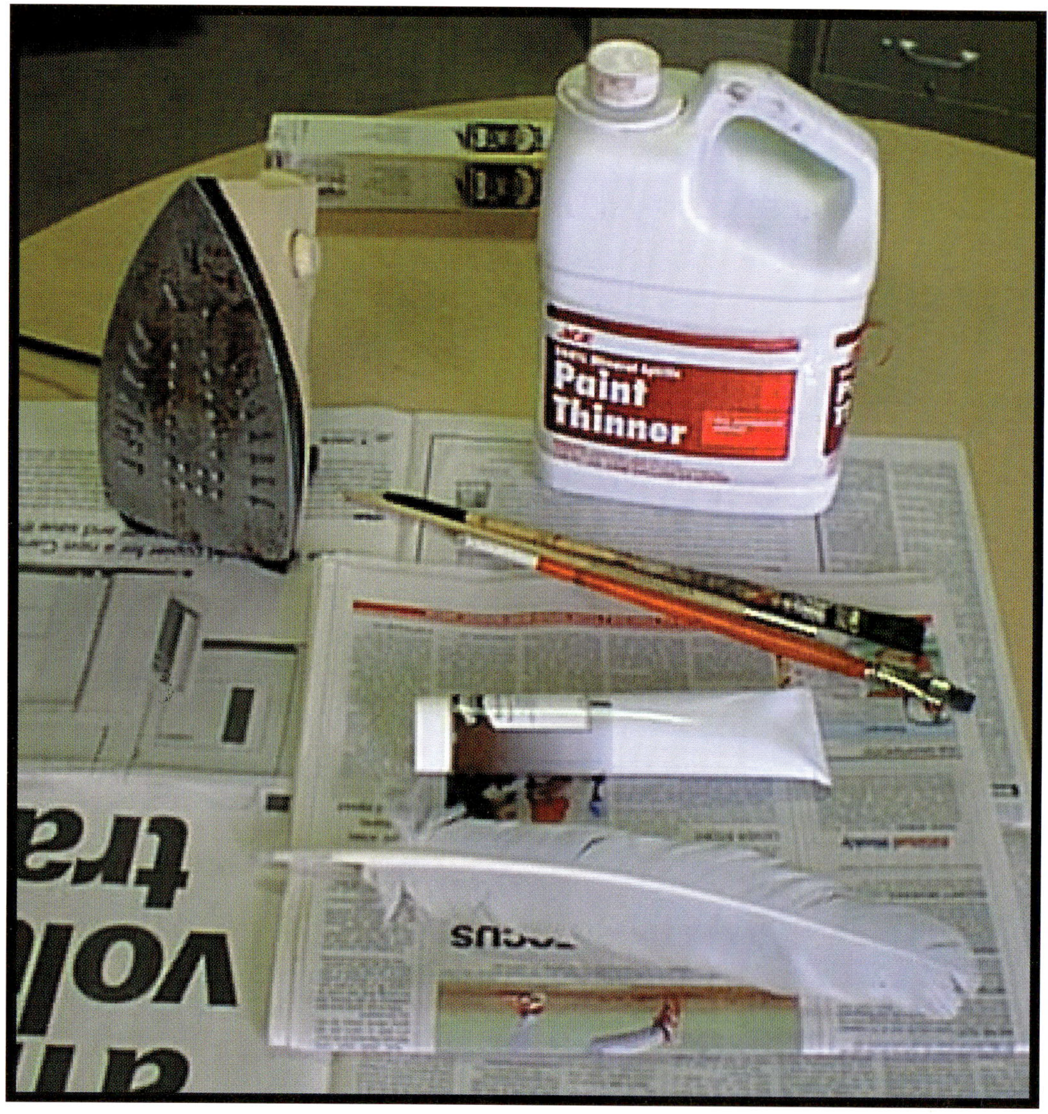

List of materials

1. Burnt umber oil paint
2. Black umber oil paint
3. Various brushes
4. Thinner
5. Feathers
6. Variable Heat Iron

Anatomy of a Feather

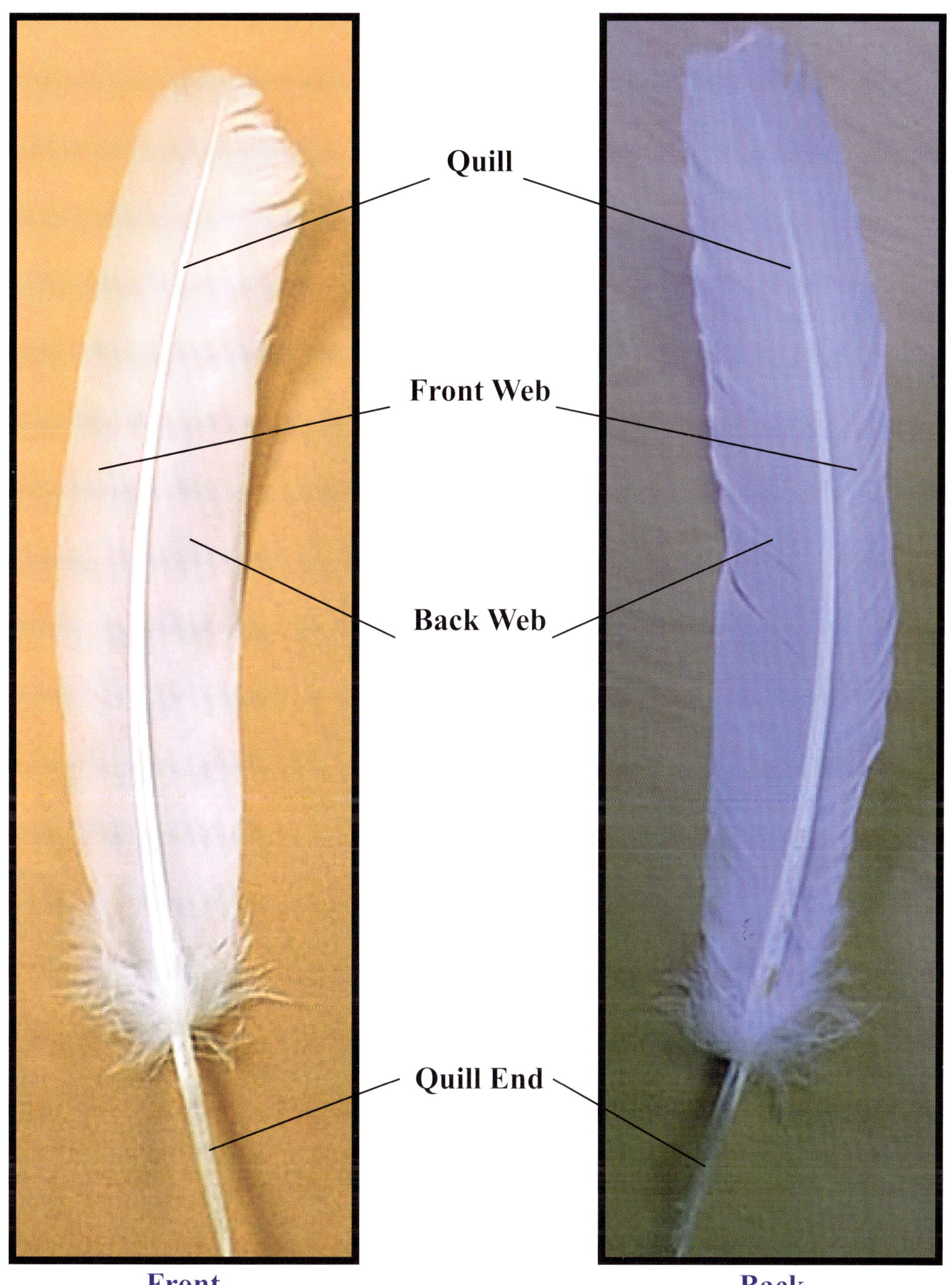

Straightening Feathers

Before any painting can begin the feathers need to be straightened, each feather has two curves, one parallel with the webbing, and one perpendicular to the webbing; each feather needs to be straightened in both directions.

You will know if you have done it right if the feather will lay flat on the table and have the quill run in a straight line.

Steps

1. Heat the iron to 4 or wool.

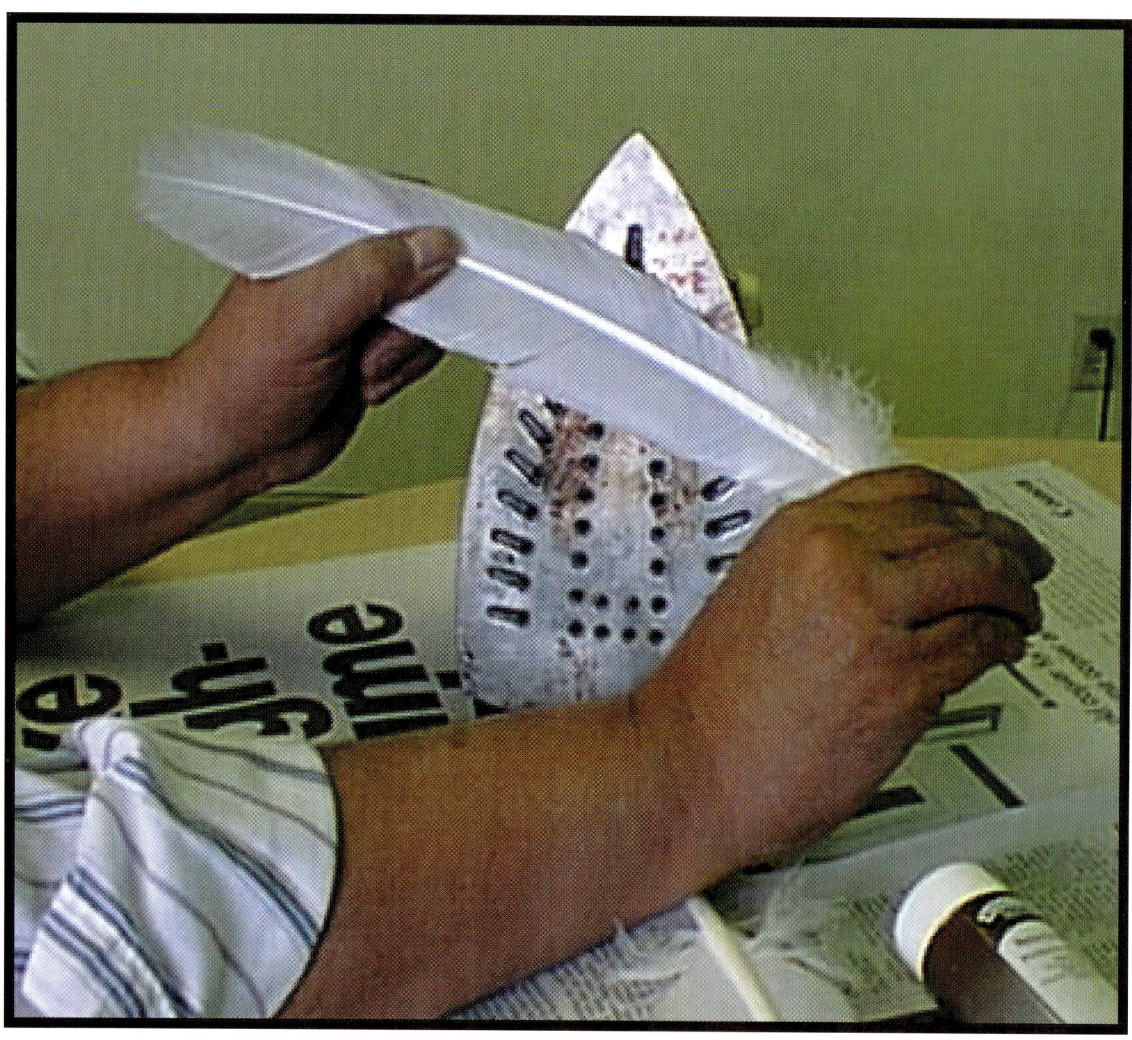

2. Once the iron is hot, place the quill part of the feather on the iron starting towards the thicker part of the quill.

3. Hold the feather both above and below the spot that you are heating.
4. You should heat it to the point that you almost can't hold it.

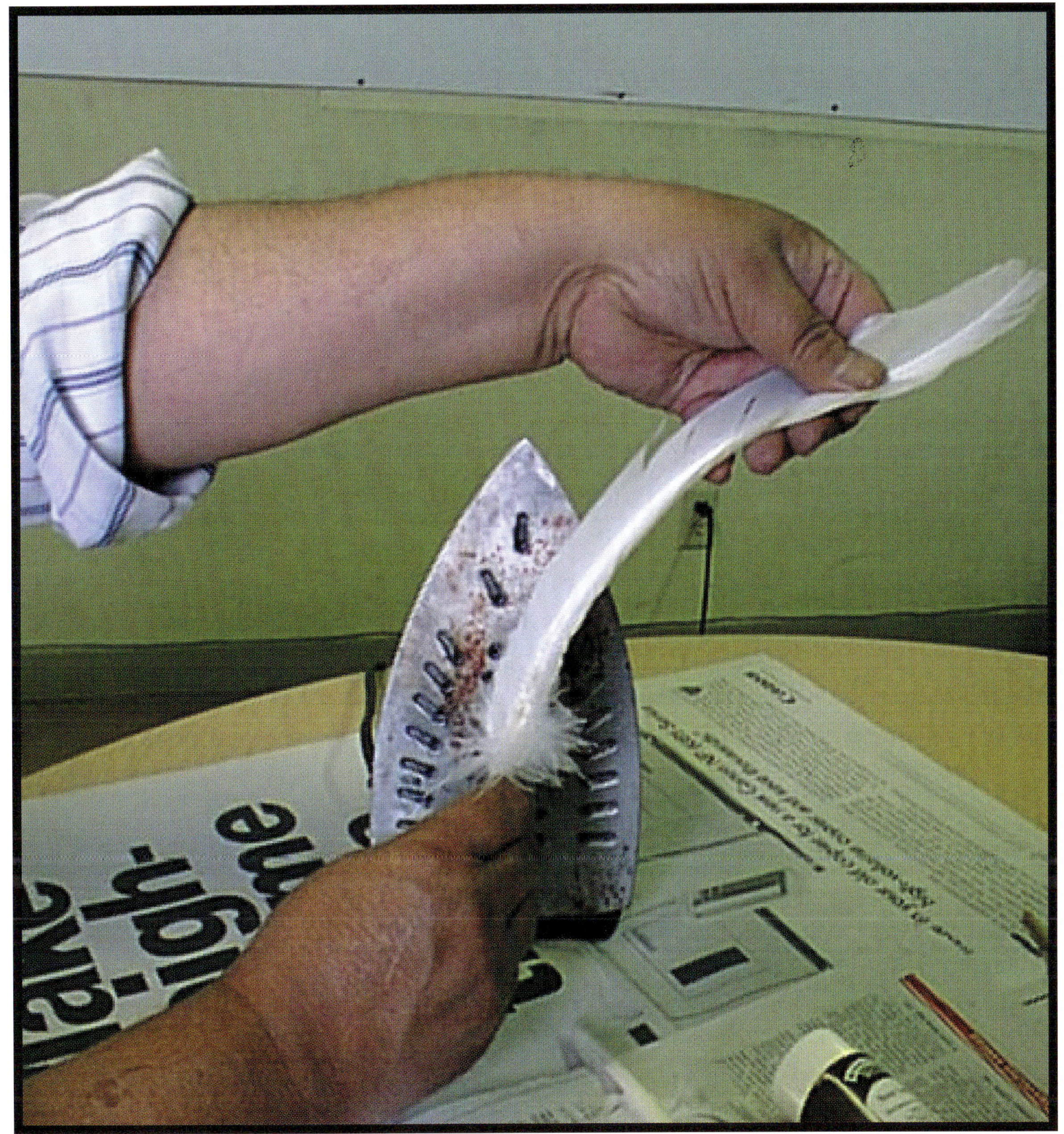

5. Bend the feather in the opposite direction of its natural curve and hold till it keeps it's shape.
6. Move up the shaft of the quill until you have straightened the entire feather.
7. As you work your way up the feather make sure that you straighten both curves (front to back and side to side).

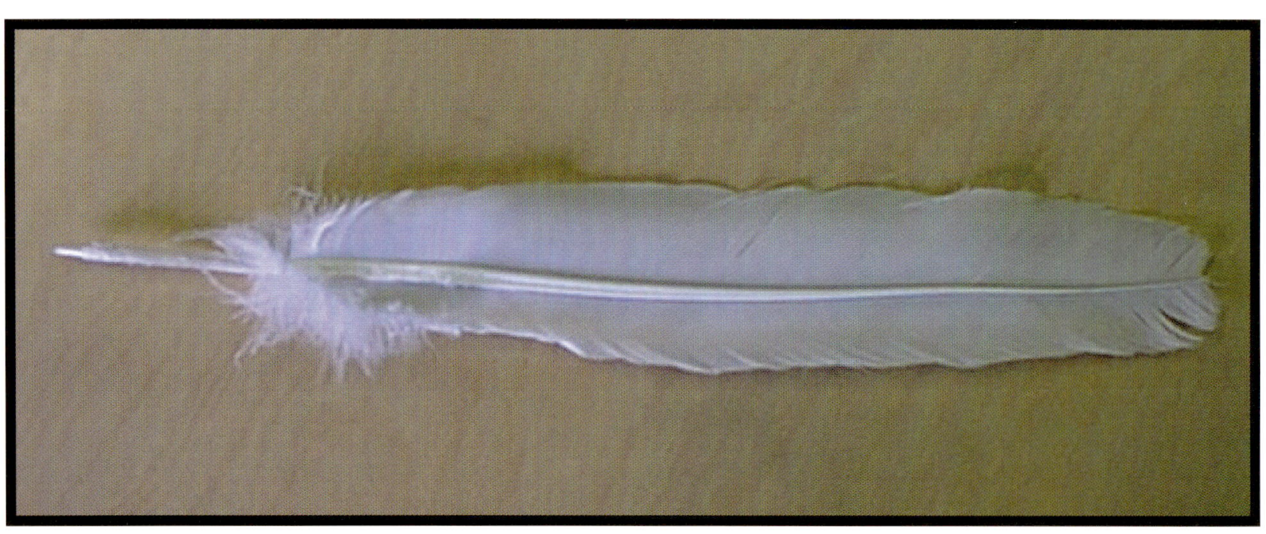

Occasionally you will find that you need to make two passes over the iron to remove all of the curve. Humidity will sometimes bring back the natural curve and some feathers may need to be straightened more than once.

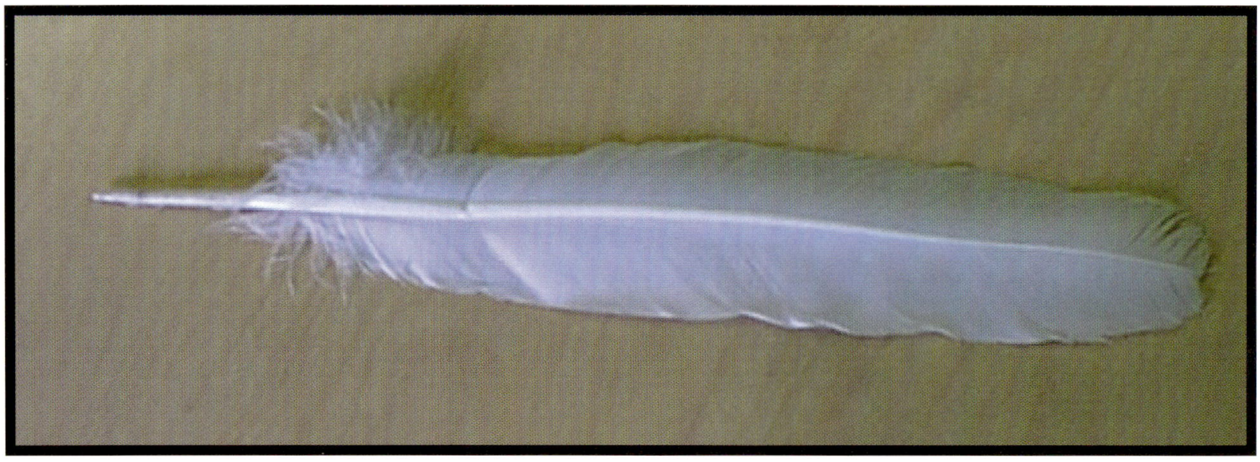

Painting

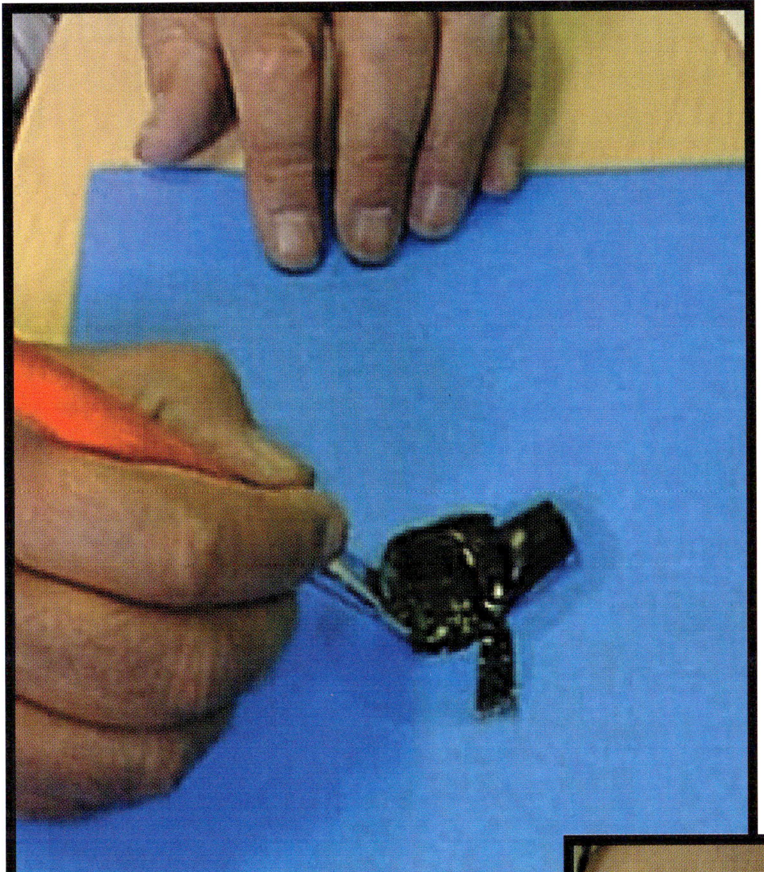

Using burnt umber and ivory black oil paint we first have to mix them according to how brown or black you want your feather to be. The more burnt umber the browner the feather will look, the more black that's added the more brown black it will become.

Using just black or just burnt umber makes the feather look unnatural. A good mixture resulting in a natural looking dark feather is a 50-50 blend.

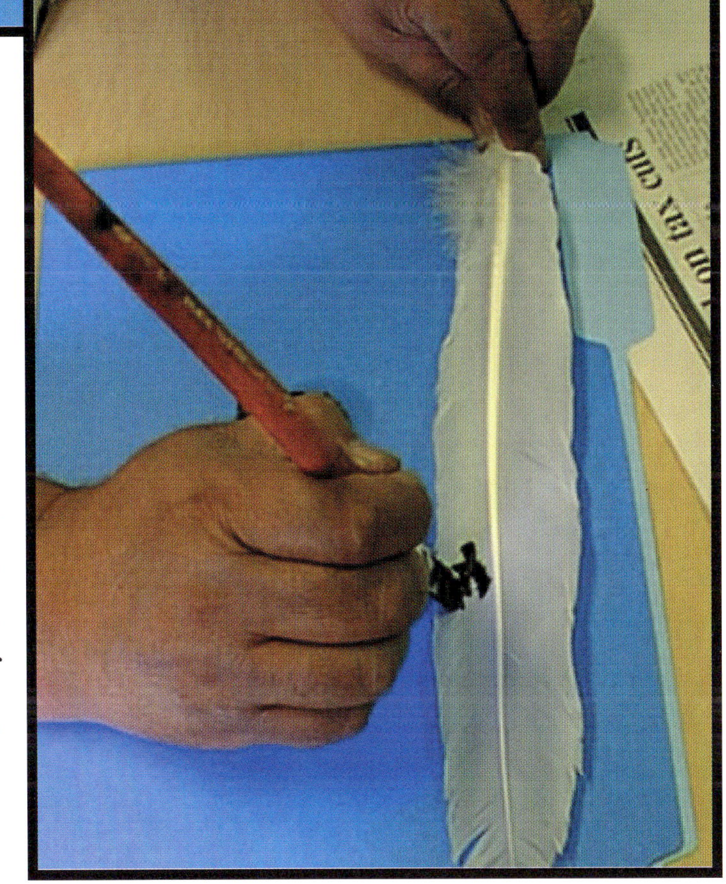

Thin part of your color blend by adding a thinner. Thinned paint should not be of a consistency that will bleed when applied to the web of the feather. It is good to have a scrap feather on hand to test your paint consistency.

On the back side of the feather begin painting the edge of the feather design. Doing your initial painting on the back side of the feather allows the paint to penetrate the web better.

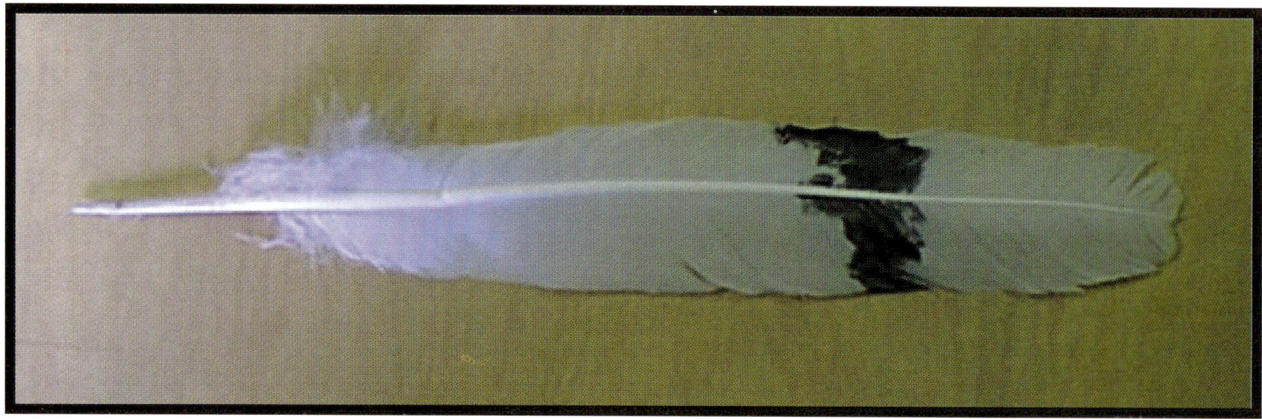

When the feather is turned over you can see that the paint has gone through the web and that the top of the feather has the same design as you painted on the back. This shows that your paint has thoroughly colored the web.

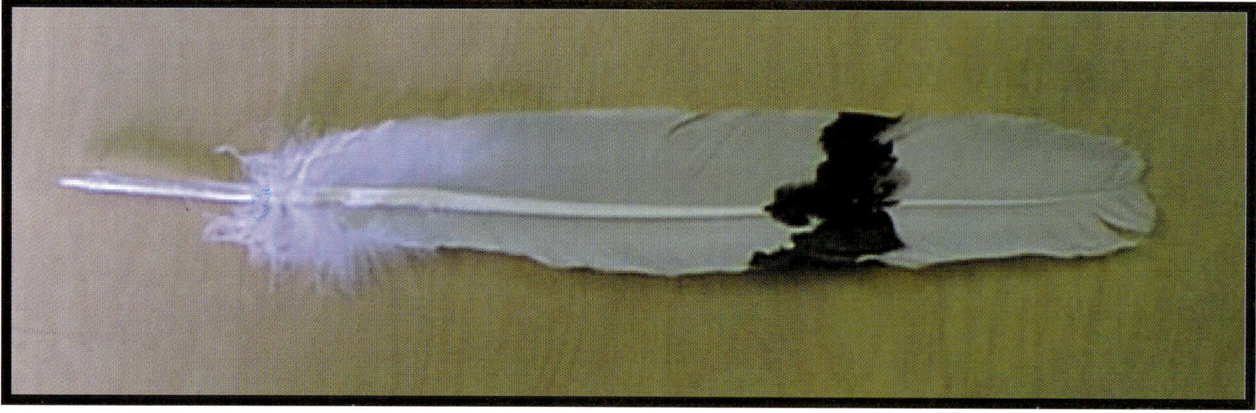

Note that the design on the front web is always lower than that on the back web. To look natural the lower edge of the design must be irregular.

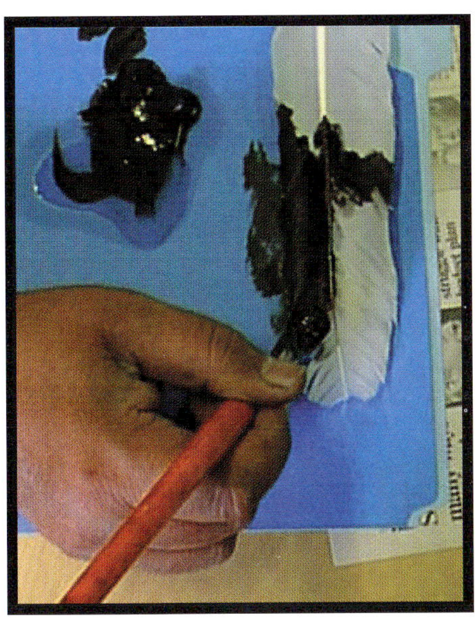

Working on the back side of the feather, put a coat of paint from your design edge to the tip of the feather.

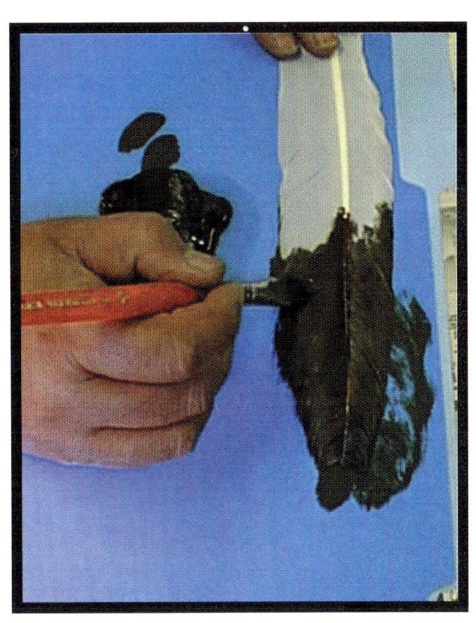

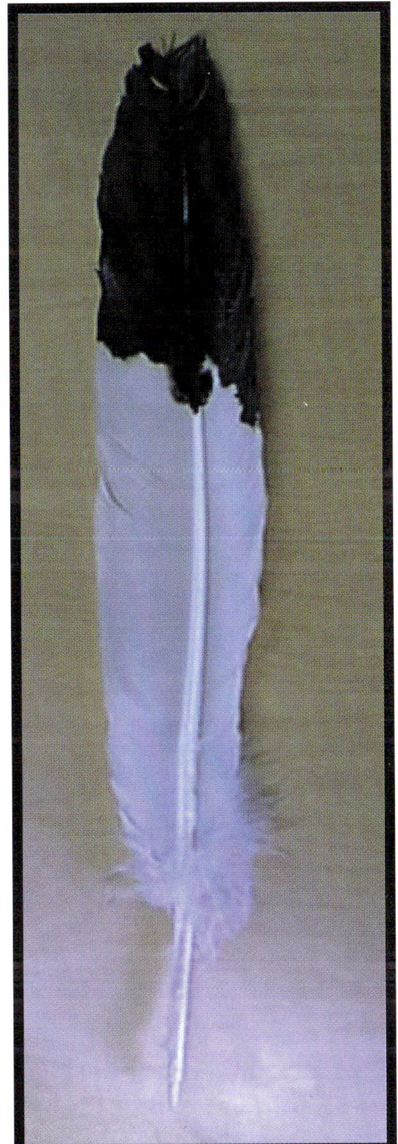

Turn the feather over and do the same to the front of the feather. The feather tip should be uniformly dark in appearance but if you hold it up to the light you should see some variation in your color.

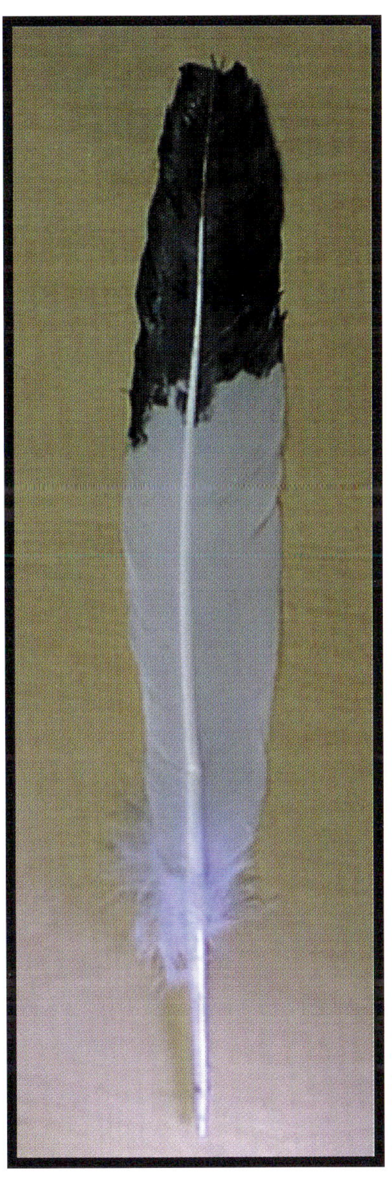

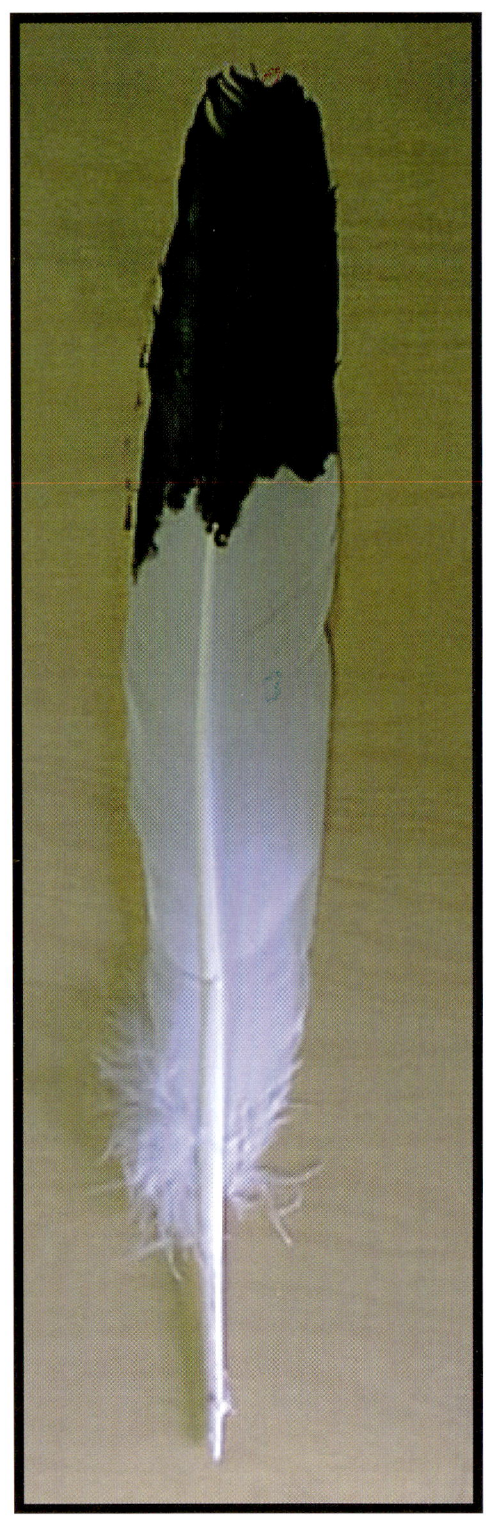

This is how your feather should look at this point.

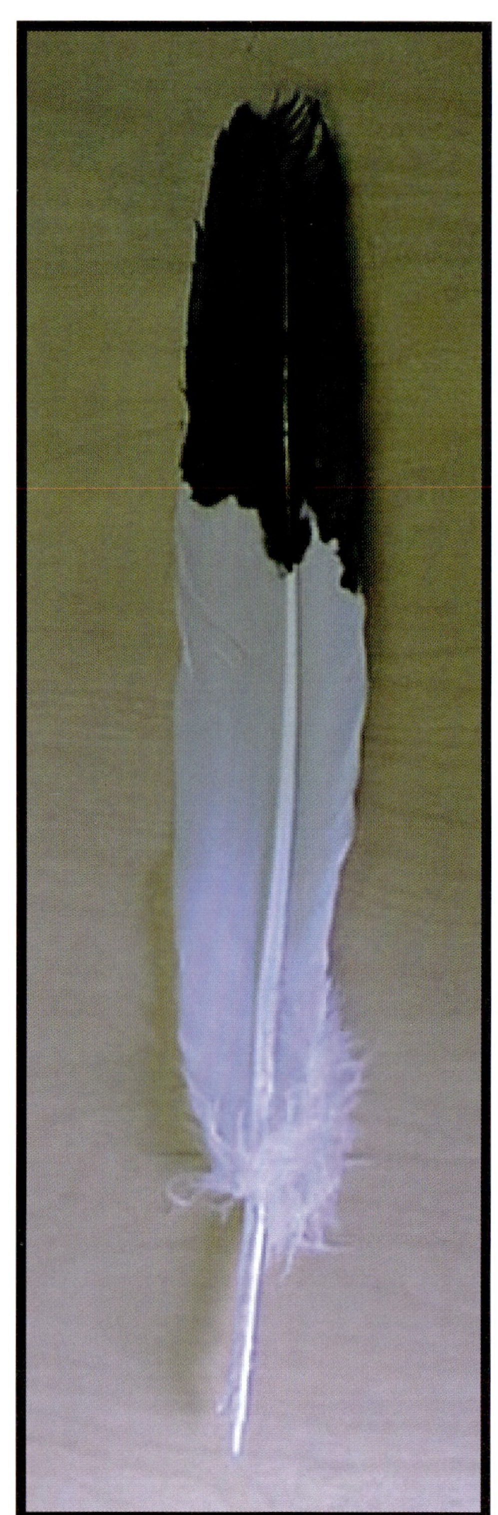

Detailing and Finishing

A variety of brush types are valuable but not necessary. At least one brush should be fairly stiff. This brush is used like a stencil brush and will create a texture on the feather. Flat and fine brushes can be used to create larger spots and shapes.

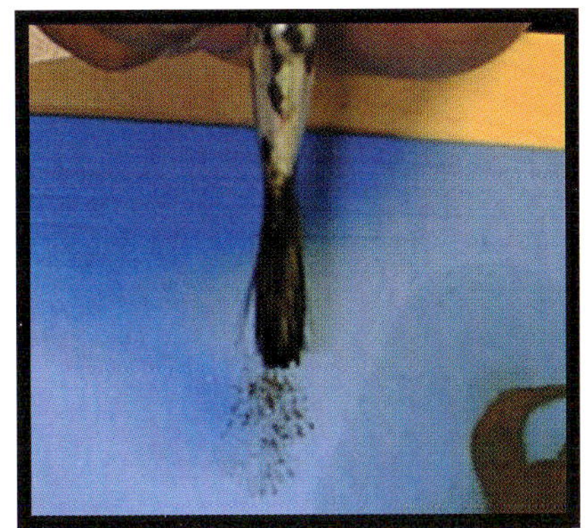

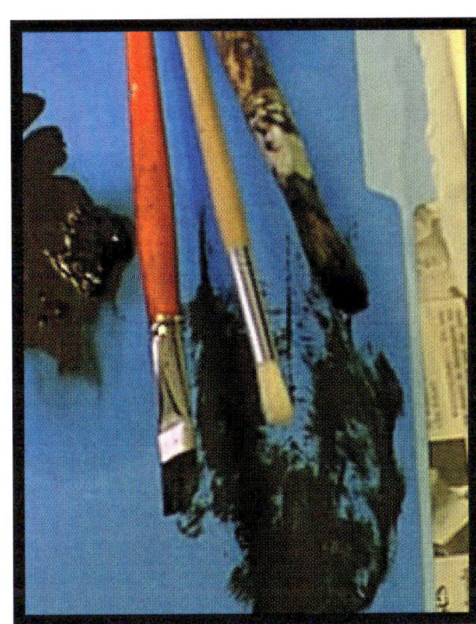

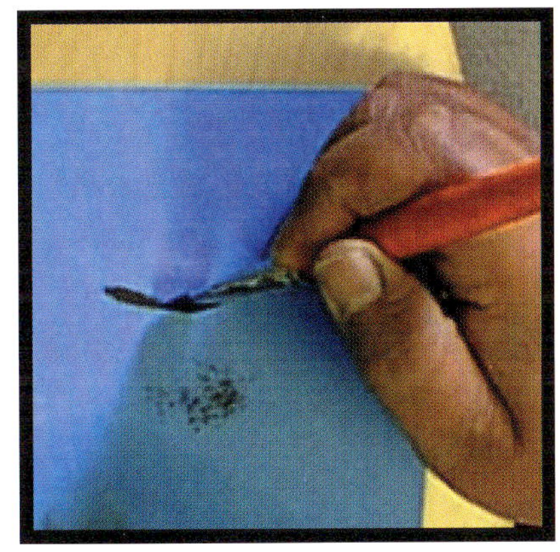

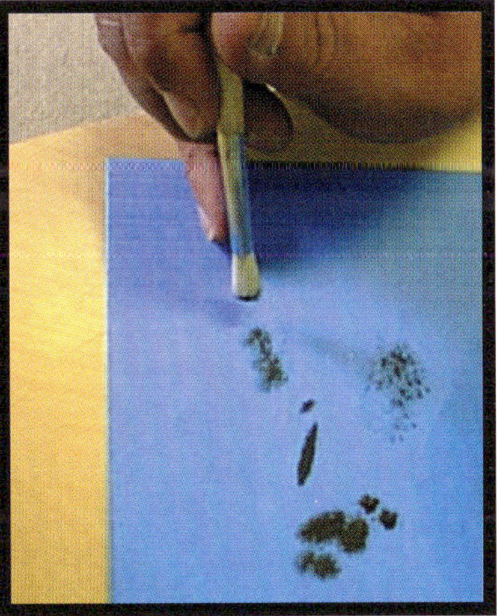

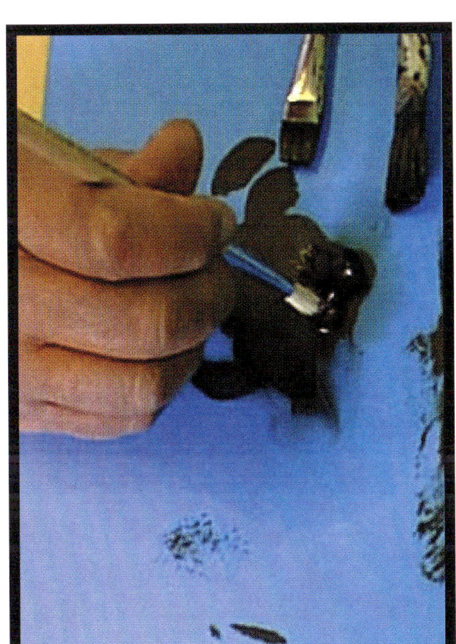

Paint used in detailing should be used straight from the tube. If thinned it should never be thin enough to bleed when applied to the web.

Use your detailing brush strokes to apply textures and shapes to your feather; apply these on the front of the feather. It is good to use a model or photograph when applying details.

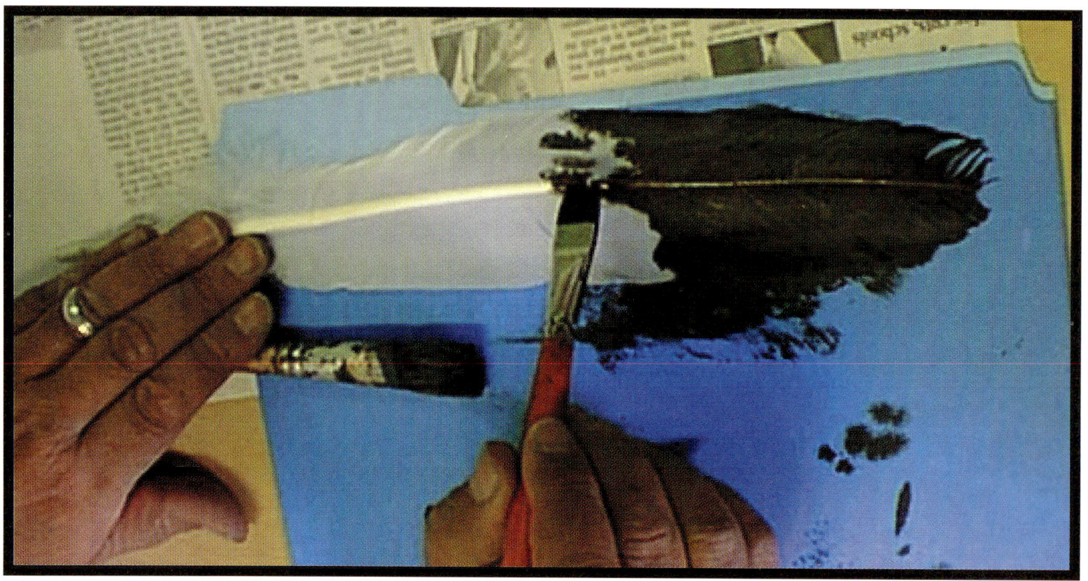

Using a stiff brush, stipple a texture that follows the edge of your design and overlaps the white of the feather and your colored design. This blends the edges of your design making them softer and more natural. Remember that like the design, this texture is lower on the front web than on the back web. Turn the feather over and lightly paint your details on the back of the feather.

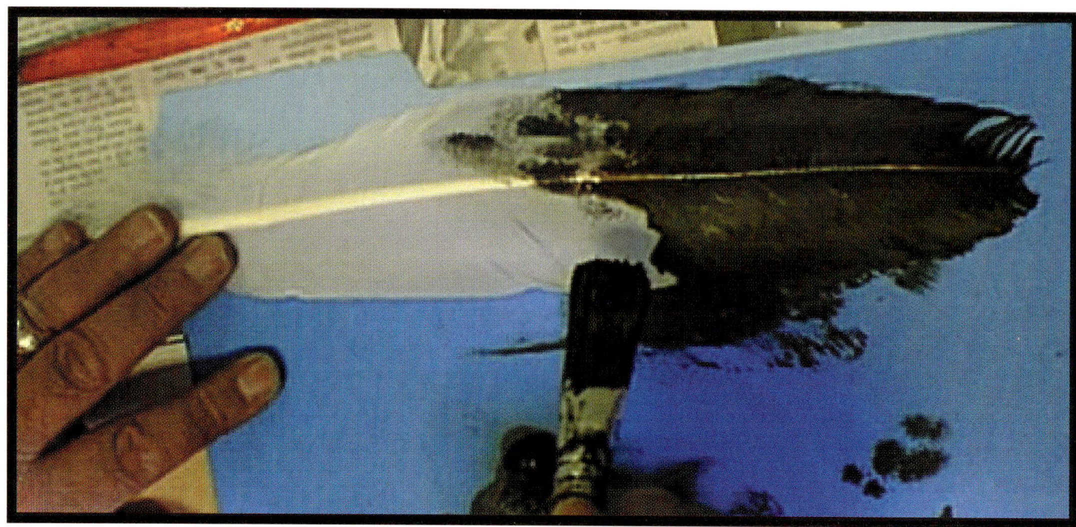

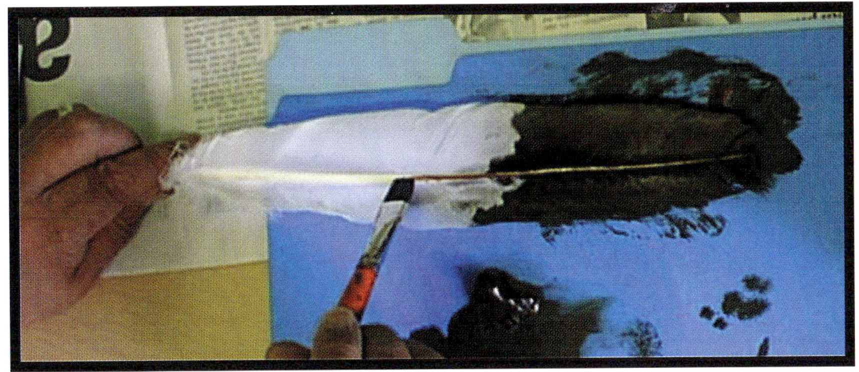

On the back side of the feather, paint the quill stem about 2/3 of the way down from the tip. This doesn't have to be heavy.

Turn the feather over and paint the front of the quill down to about 2 inches below the design. Paint the quill heavily enough to cover it sufficiently .

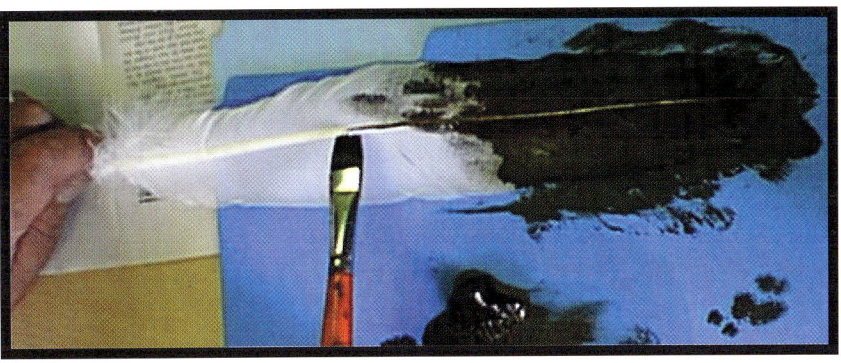

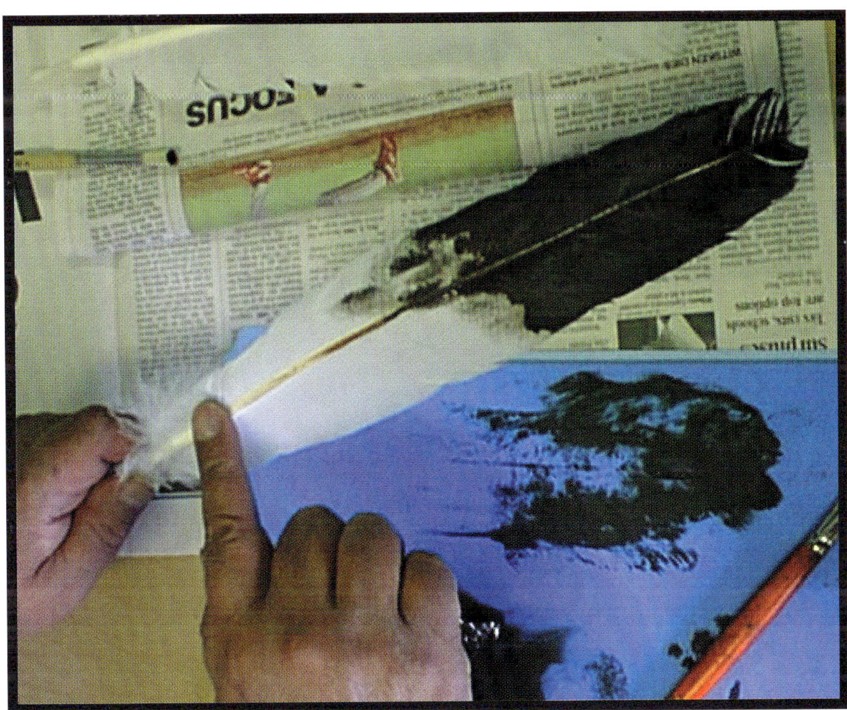

With your fingertip blend the paint on the quill down towards the quill tip. This will cause the color to gradually fade as it moves toward the quill tip.

Note: The quill is very difficult to get to hold the paint, sanding it lightly gives a better surface for the paint to adhere to. Sometimes more than one coat needs to be applied.

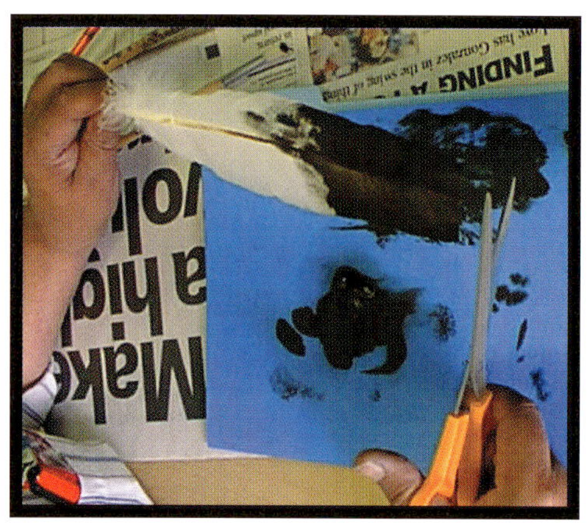

Clip the feather so that you remove the tip for about 1 inch, so that any of the tip that is too flimsy is removed. Clip this straight across the feather.

Holding the feather so that you cut towards the quill end, round the tip. Cutting towards the quill end creates a smoother edge.

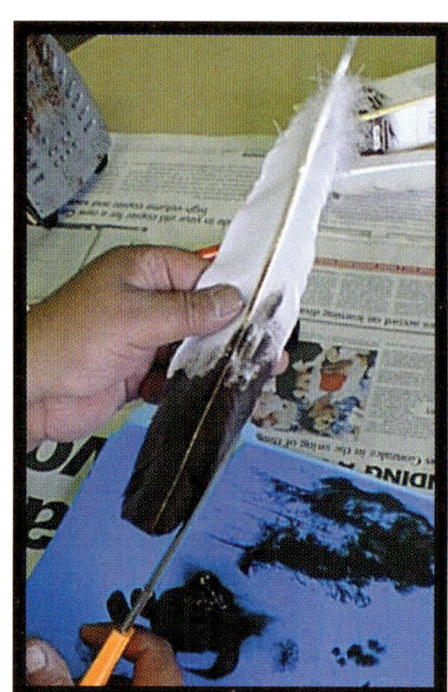

The tip should be rounded not pointed. Check your models and photographs so that your trim looks natural.

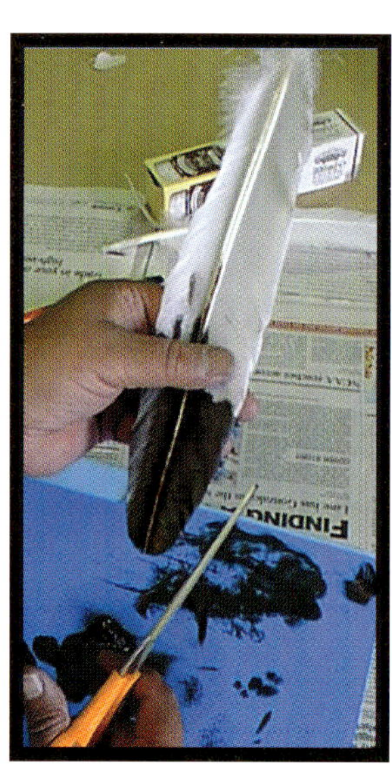

Turning the feather over enables you to trim the other side and still cut towards the quill end.

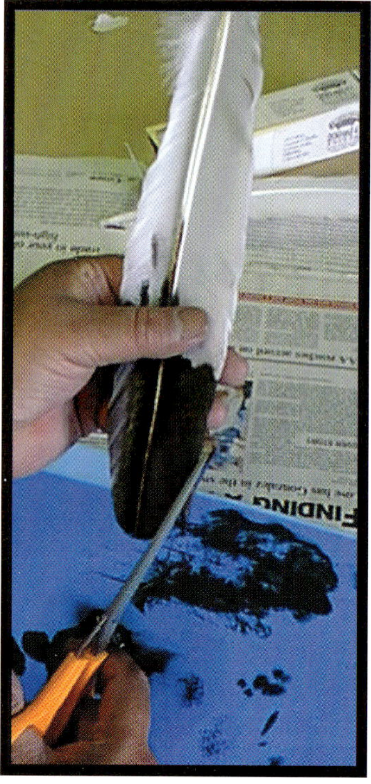

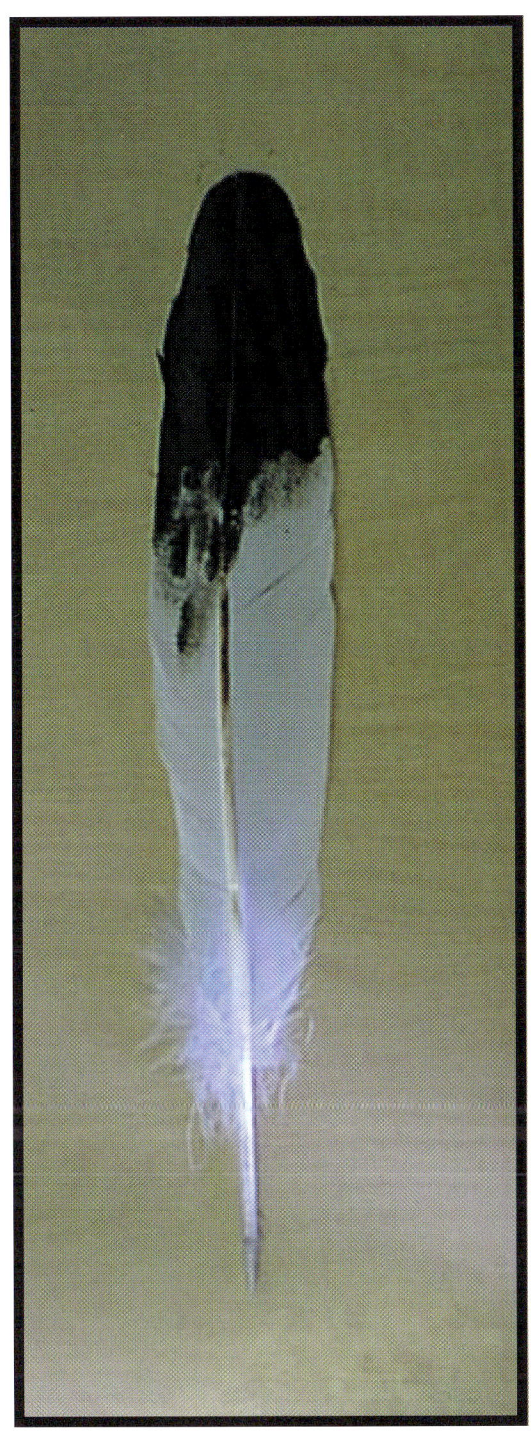

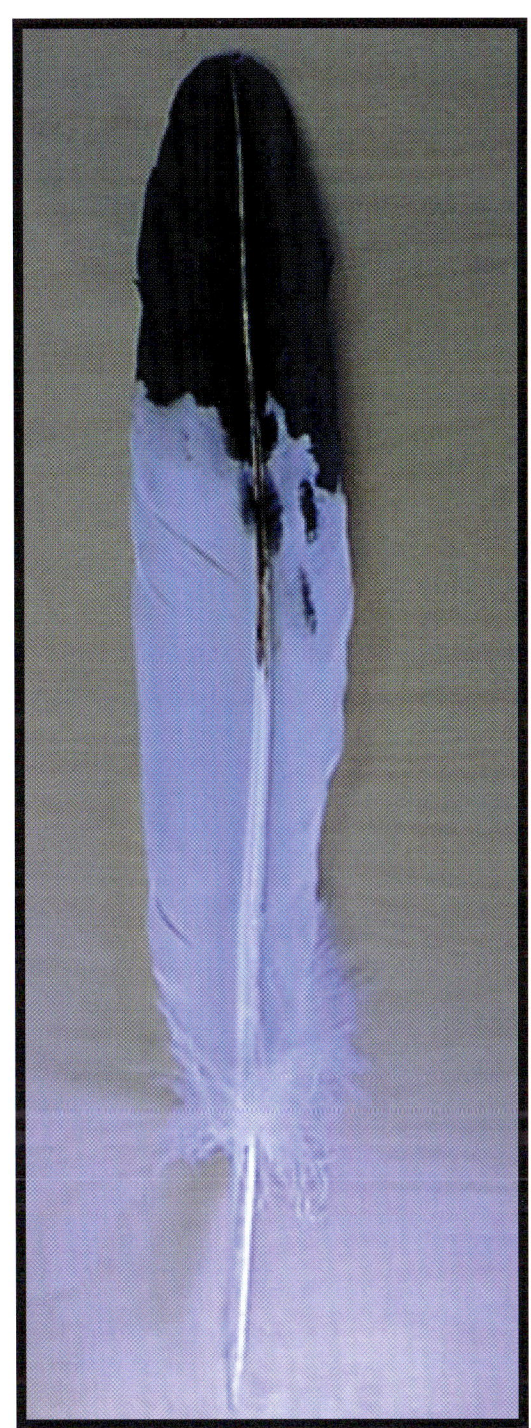

Summary

You can see that by using these directions you should have a feather that can be used in making any number of Native American artifact reproductions. You have something that is both convincing and legal.

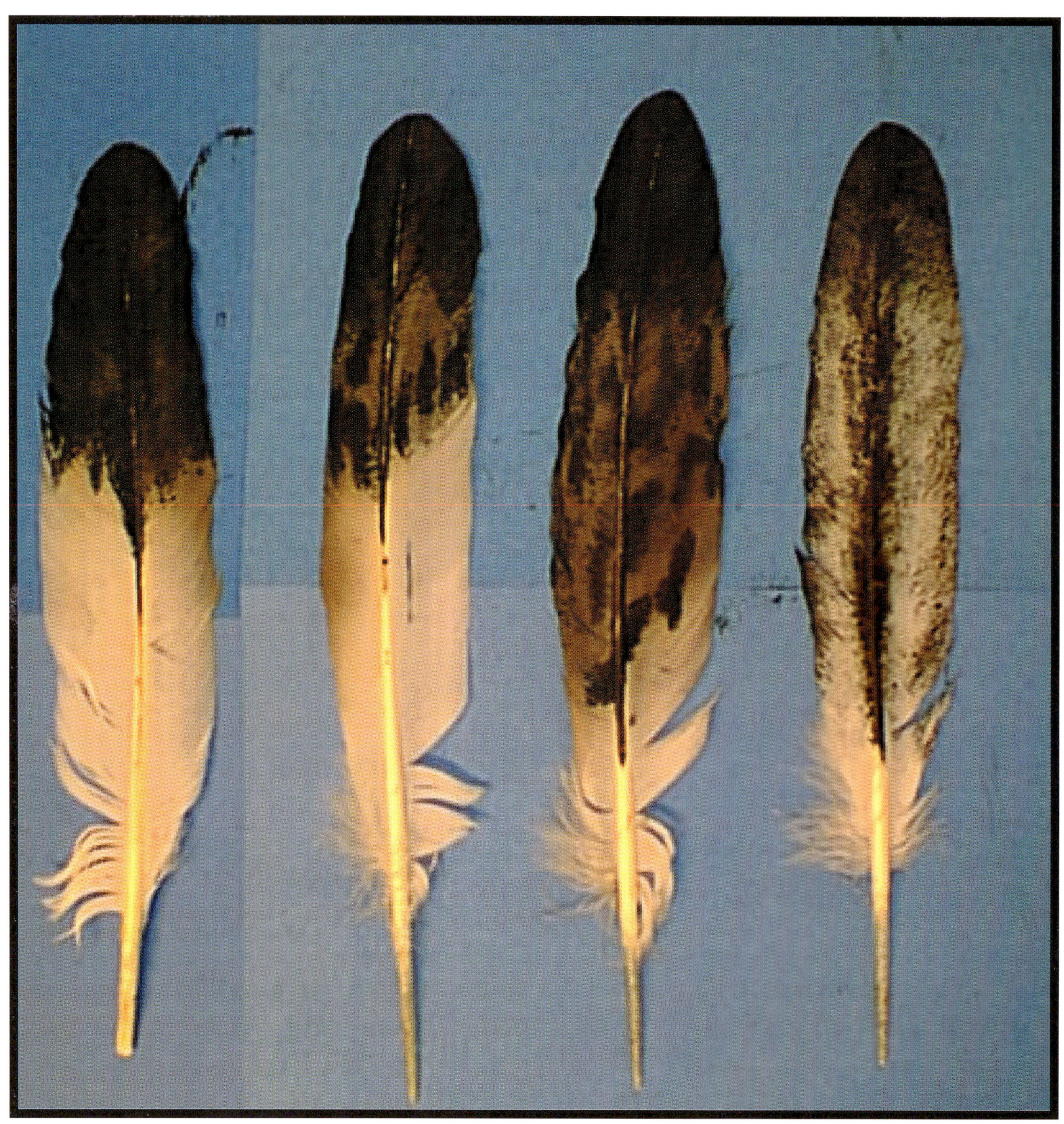

Now that you have the basics of developing a feather, you may want to simulate feathers from various phases of the Golden and Bald Eagles.

The growth phases from both species provide distinctly different feathers, and while the basic painting approach is the same, there are distinctive differences in the patterns.

Immature Golden Eagle Feathers

The immature Golden Eagle feather is the predominantly white feather with the black tip that is usually associated with Native American crafts. It is the feather used to provide the basic instructions in the beginning portion of this book.

The characteristics of the immature Golden Eagle are the distinctive light and dark sections with little or no coloration between the two. As in all eagle feathers the designs on the front web go lower on the feather than those on the back web.

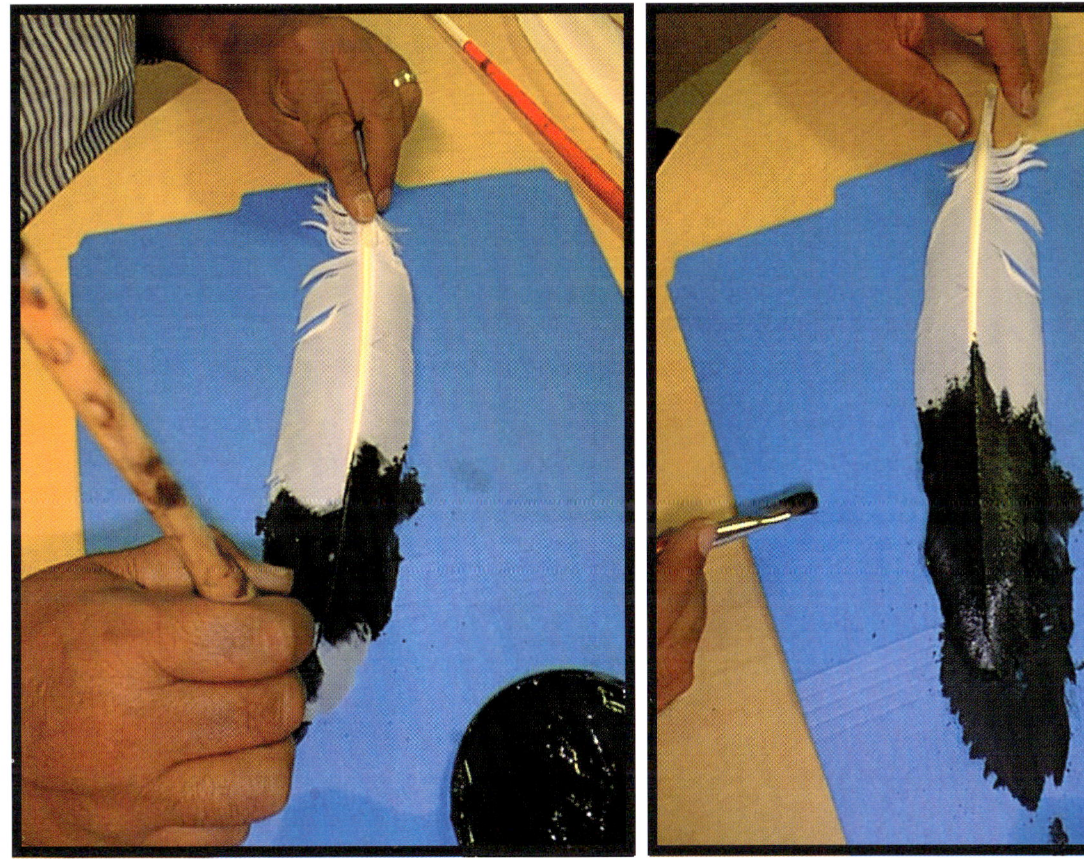

The front and back of the immature feather are both strongly colored and you need to begin your painting on the back side of the feather.

Remember that the painting will look more natural if the edges between the dark and light sections are not too sharp.

Intermediate Golden Eagle Feathers

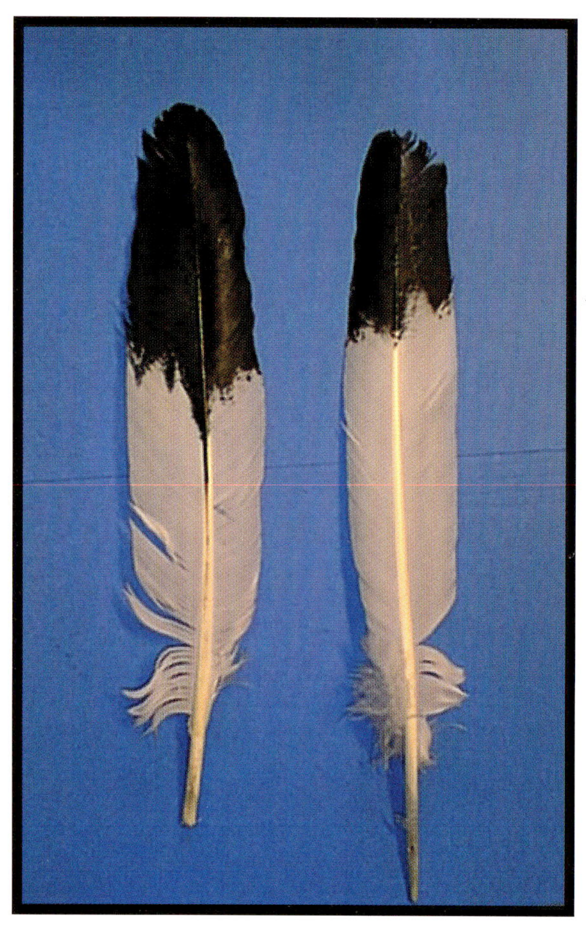

The intermediate Golden Eagle feather has a dark section at the top similar to the immature feather. The dark section at the very top is shaped and colored strongly on both sides as it is on the immature. The major difference is that in the intermediate feather the dark section is shorter.

In nature, as the eagle matures, the lower edge of the dark shape is replaced by a broken pattern.

These broken patterns take the shape of vertical blobs that often touch each other. The overall impression of the pattern is of a zig-zag line that starts high on the back web and goes down as it reaches the front web.

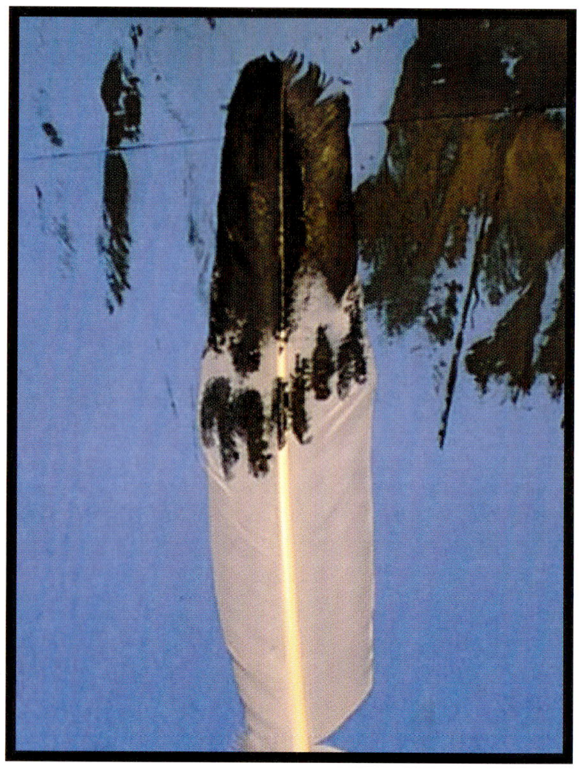

The zig-zag shapes at the bottom of the dark section are not as dark on the back of the feather as they are on the front. Although you may want to touch up the painting on the back side of the feather it is not necessary.

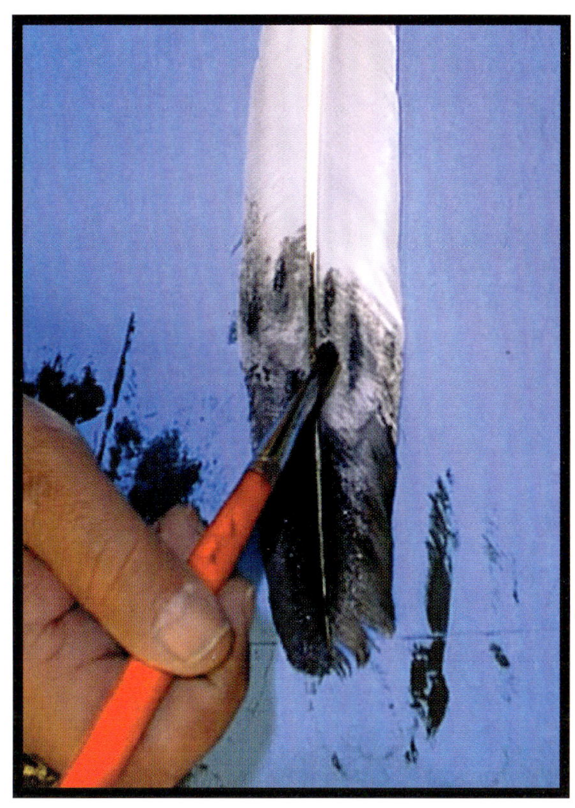

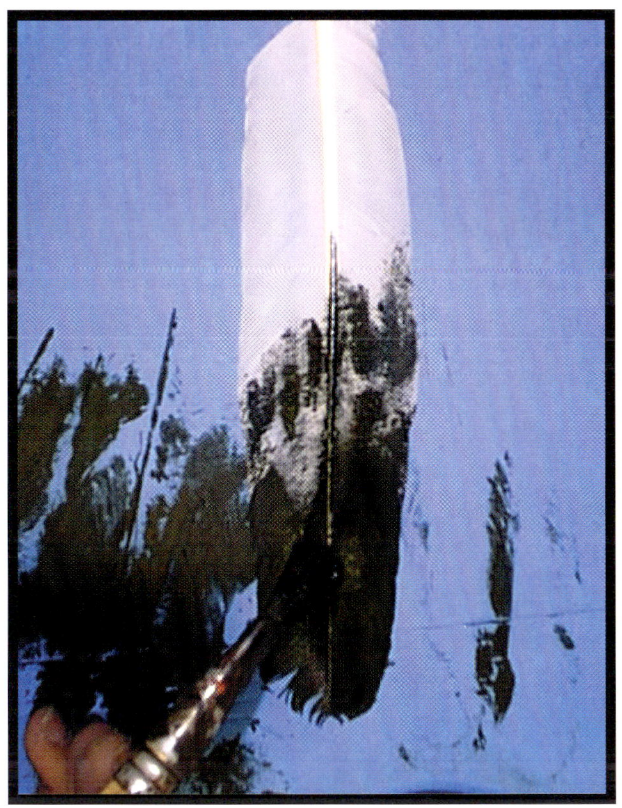

The space between the large dark section and zig-zag pattern is stippled. This stippling should lightly color the white spaces around the zig-zag pattern and the space between the pattern and the large dark section.

As you can see from the picture, the section that was just stippled has a brown cast to it. This was created using an airbrush. The airbrush need not be an expensive model. In fact an inexpensive exterior feed works best.

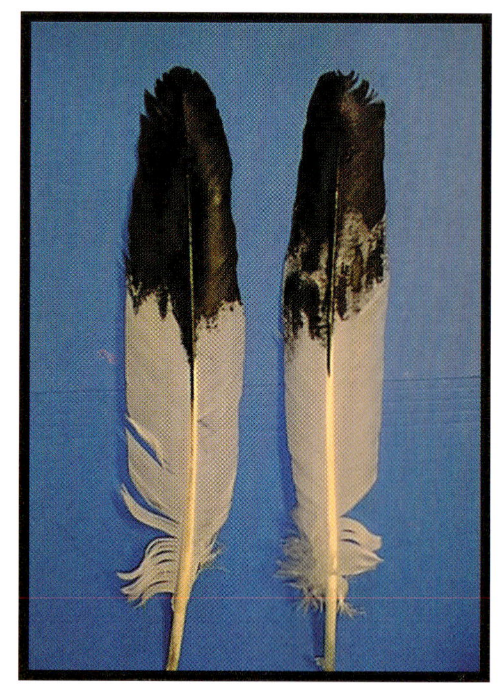

Air Brush Technique

The exterior feed is also convenient because it requires less paint preparation. The paint mixture should be about one part paint to ten parts thinner, this however needs to be experimented with.

It is also better to use a higher portion of burnt umber and very little black. The resulting color should be very thin and have a predominantly brown tone.

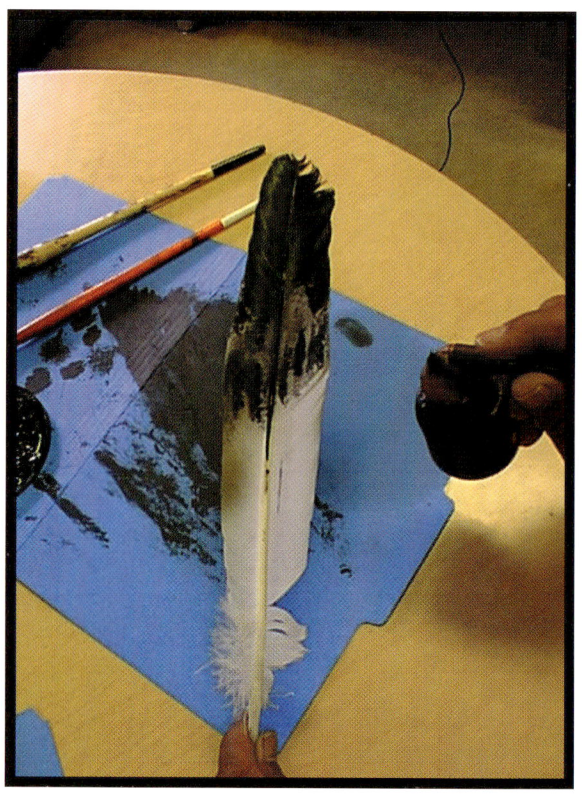

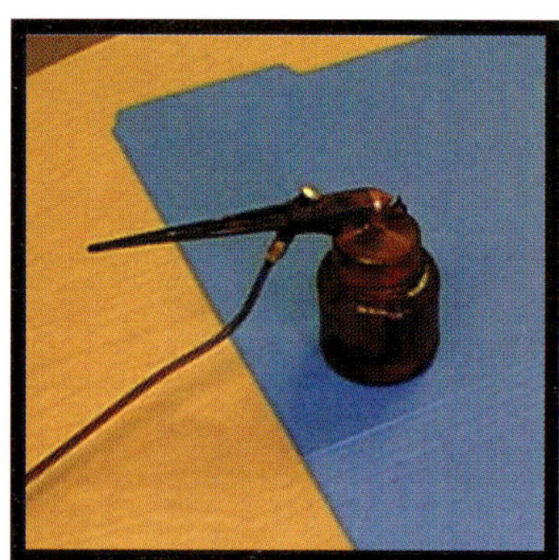

Notice that the airbrushed tone goes down the front web, fading towards the bottom.

Mature Golden Eagle Feathers

The mature Golden Eagle feather is predominantly dark. It is begun the same as the intermediate with a small dark section at the top that is again shorter than the dark section found on the immature feather.

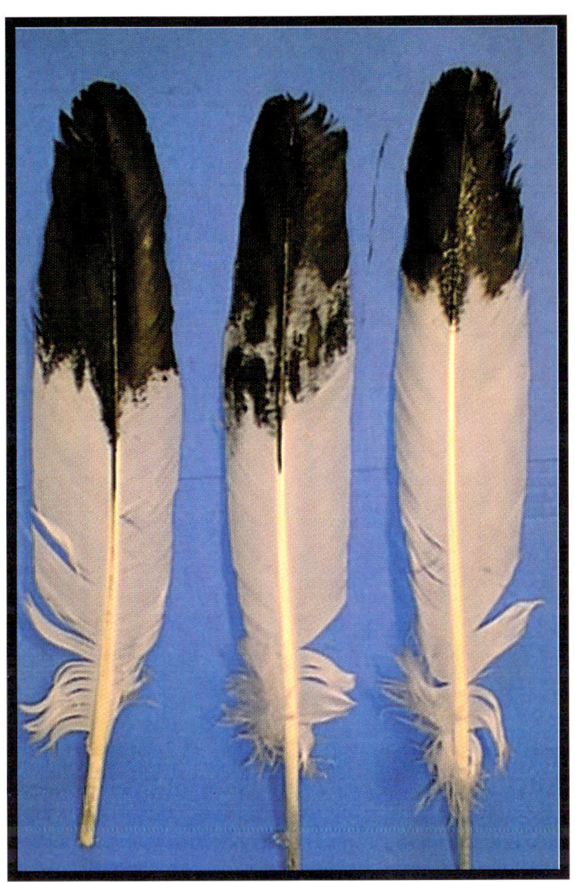

The started mature feather is on the right of the picture. The pattern on the mature is the same as that found on the intermediate feather. The difference is that the patterns continue in zig-zag, slanted rows the length of the feather. As in the intermediate feather the patterns below the large dark section do not have to be as dark on the back of the feather.

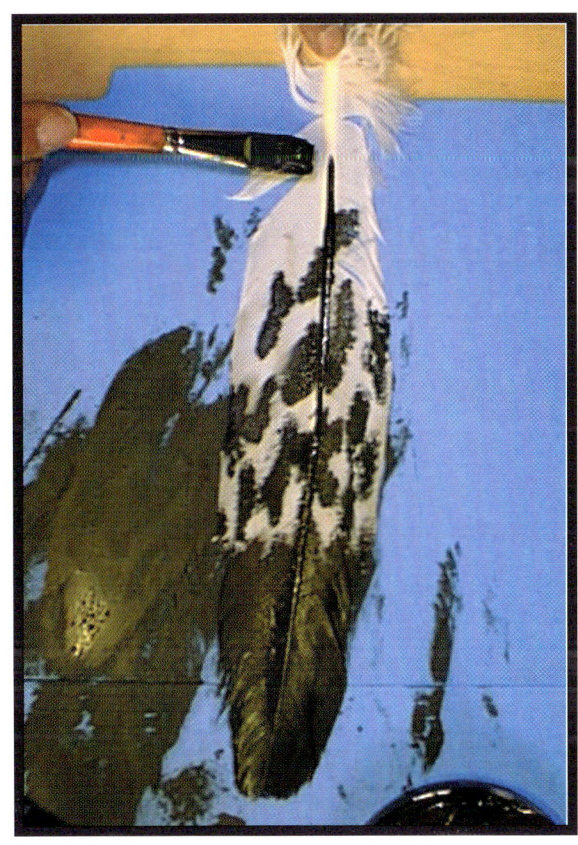

As the zig-zag patterns move down the feather they also begin closer to the quill.

Remember that the designs on the front web are lower than those on the back web.

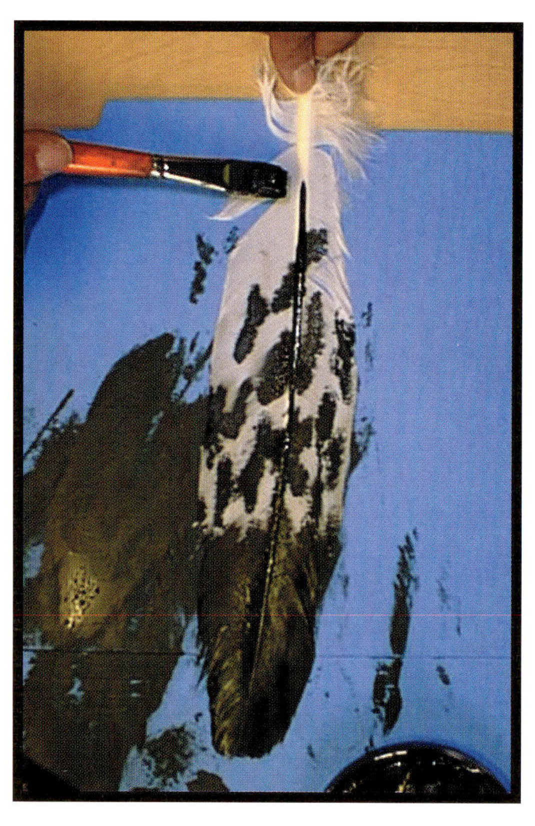

The quill is painted the entire length of the feather web.

Taper the end of the paint at the bottom by blending with your fingertip.

Remember to paint the back of the quill.

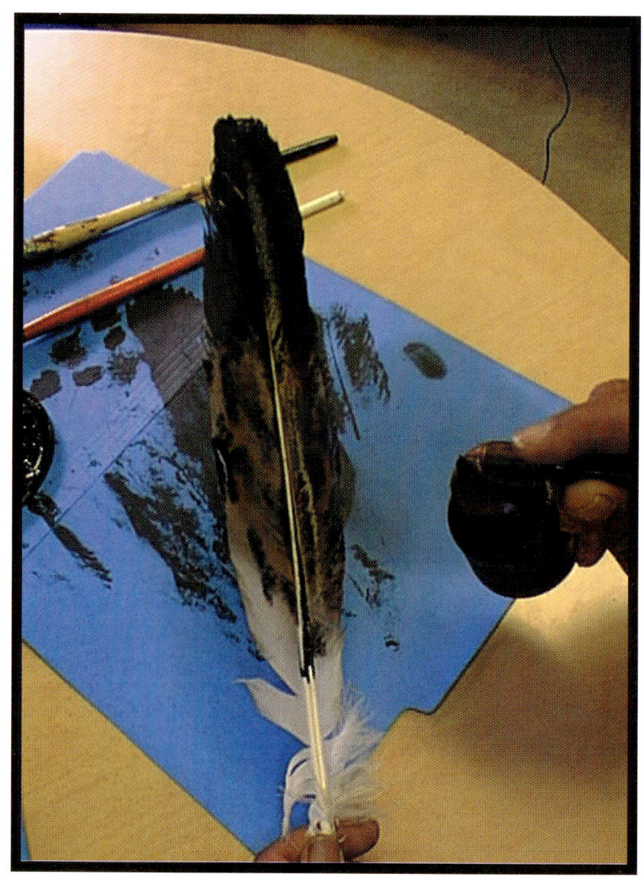

After stippling the spaces between and around the zig-zag patterns air brush the entire feather with a paint mixture similar to that used on the intermediate feather. Notice in the picture that there is a white section at the bottom of the feather and that the white section is higher on the back web and lower on the front web.

Immature Bald Eagle Feathers

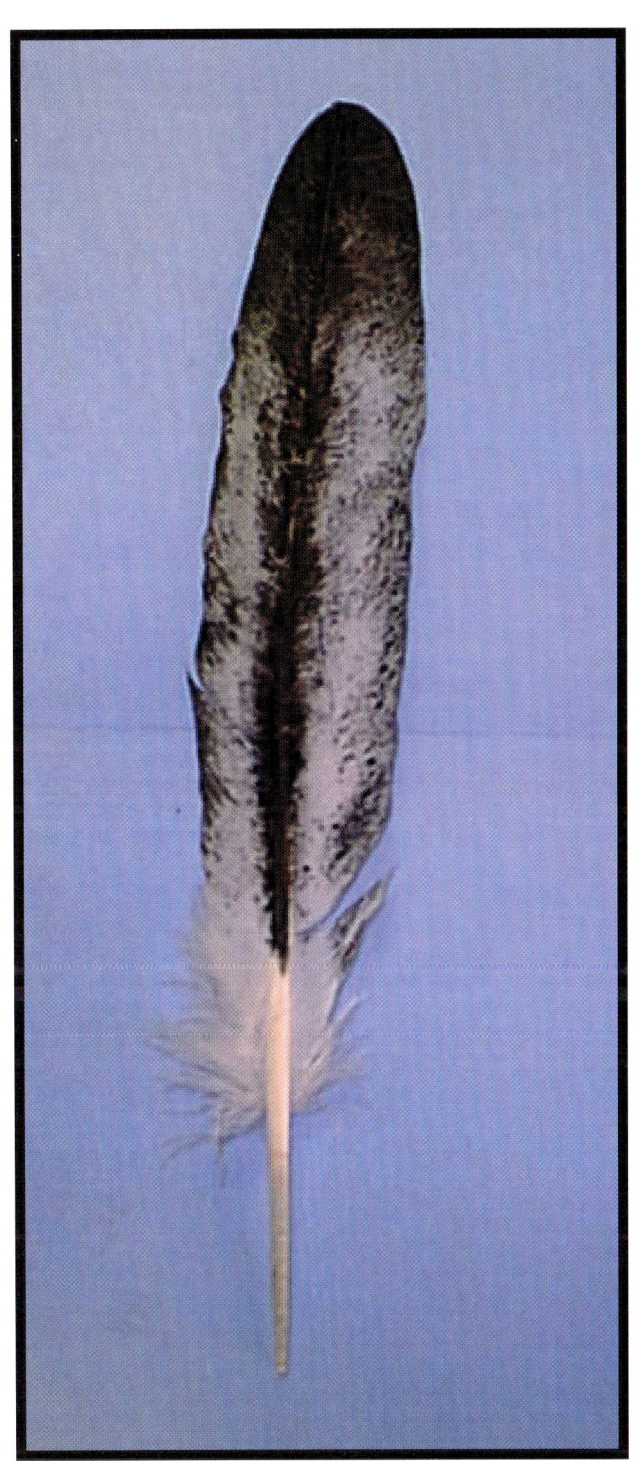

Immature Bald Eagle feathers are different from those of the Golden Eagle in that as the bird matures the feathers get whiter. The patterns on the immature bald eagle are heaviest around the quill and the outer edges of the web.

The entire design is made using a stiff brush stipple.

Notice that the stippling is darker near the quill and the tip and along the outer edges of the webs.

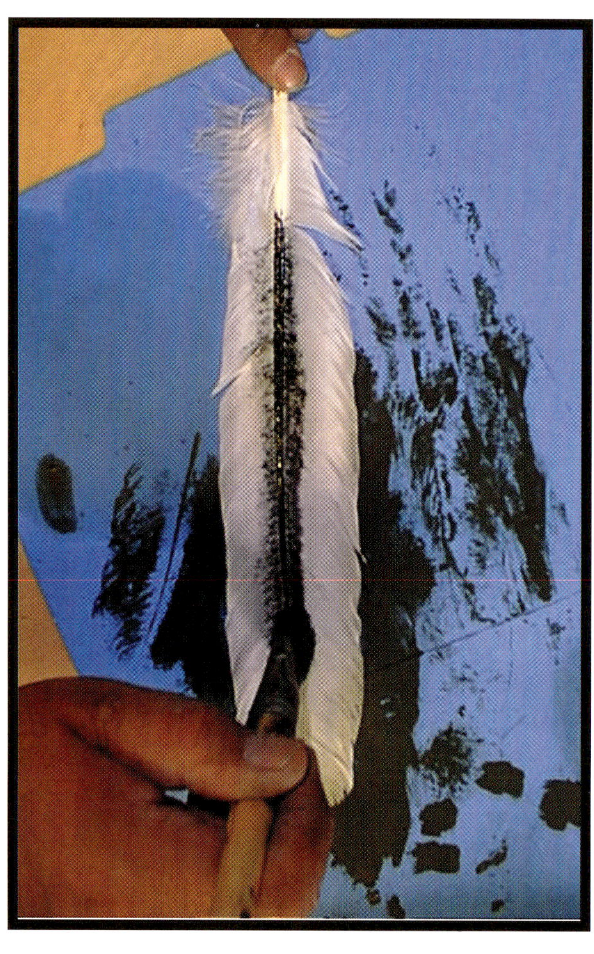

Using a stiff brush and the same color mix used on the Golden Eagle feathers begin stippling on the back side of the feather.

Work from the bottom of the feather to the tip putting on a fairly heavy stipple up the quill.

Continue stippling once you reach the tip until you have a dark band across the top of the feather. This should match the stippling around the quill in intensity.

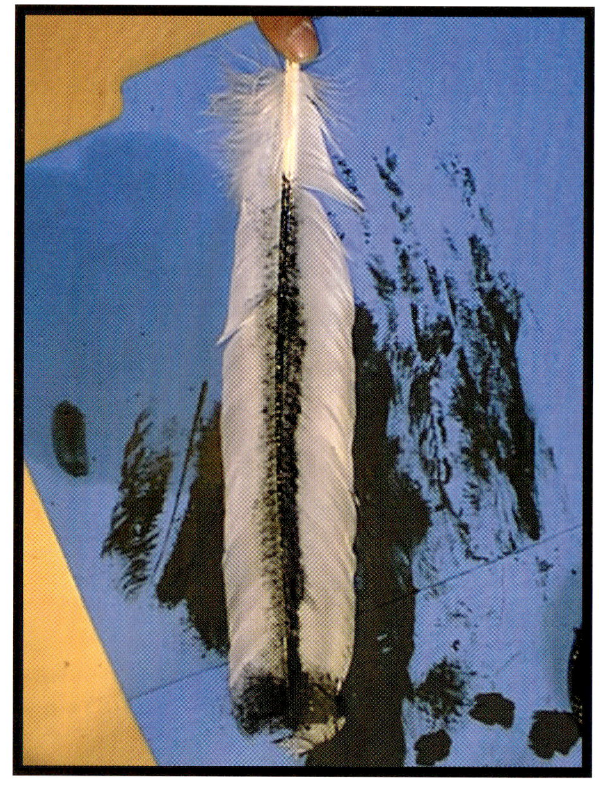

Turn the feather over and stipple the front the same way.

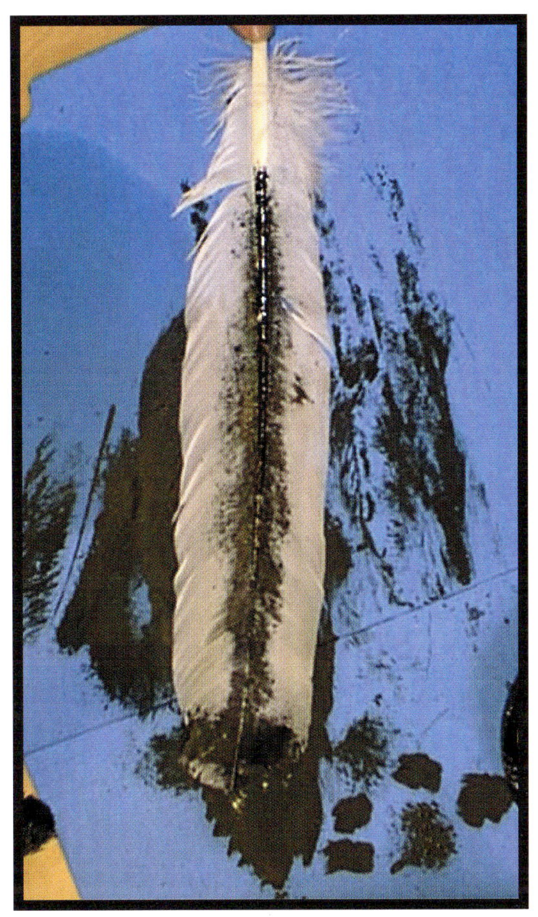

Continue the stippling along the edges of the web.

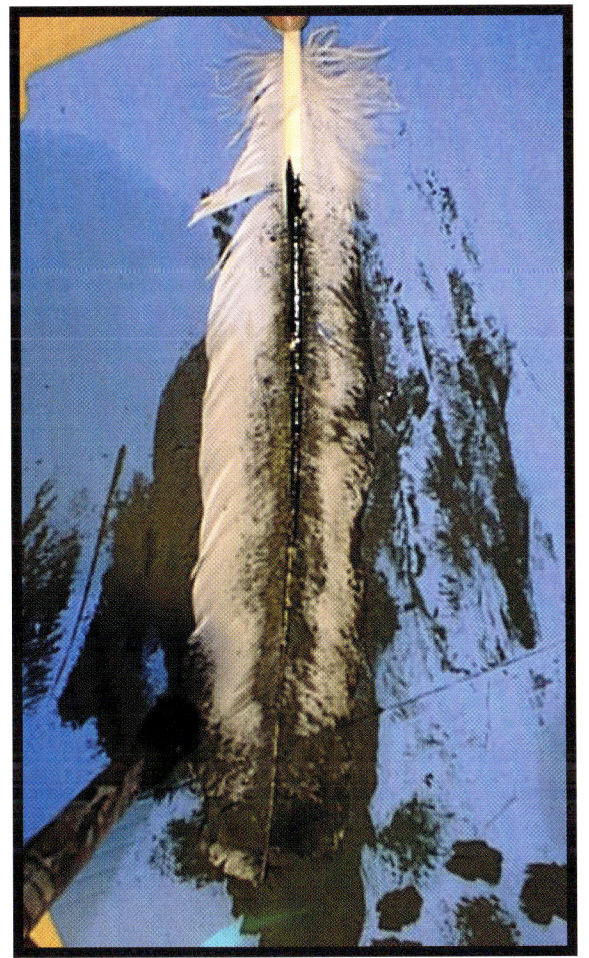

The darker and denser this pattern of stippling is, the younger the bird that will be represented.

Notice that there is a middle area between the edge of the web and the quill that is white.

These areas need to be lightly stippled. Again, the denser the stippling in this area, the younger the bird that is represented.

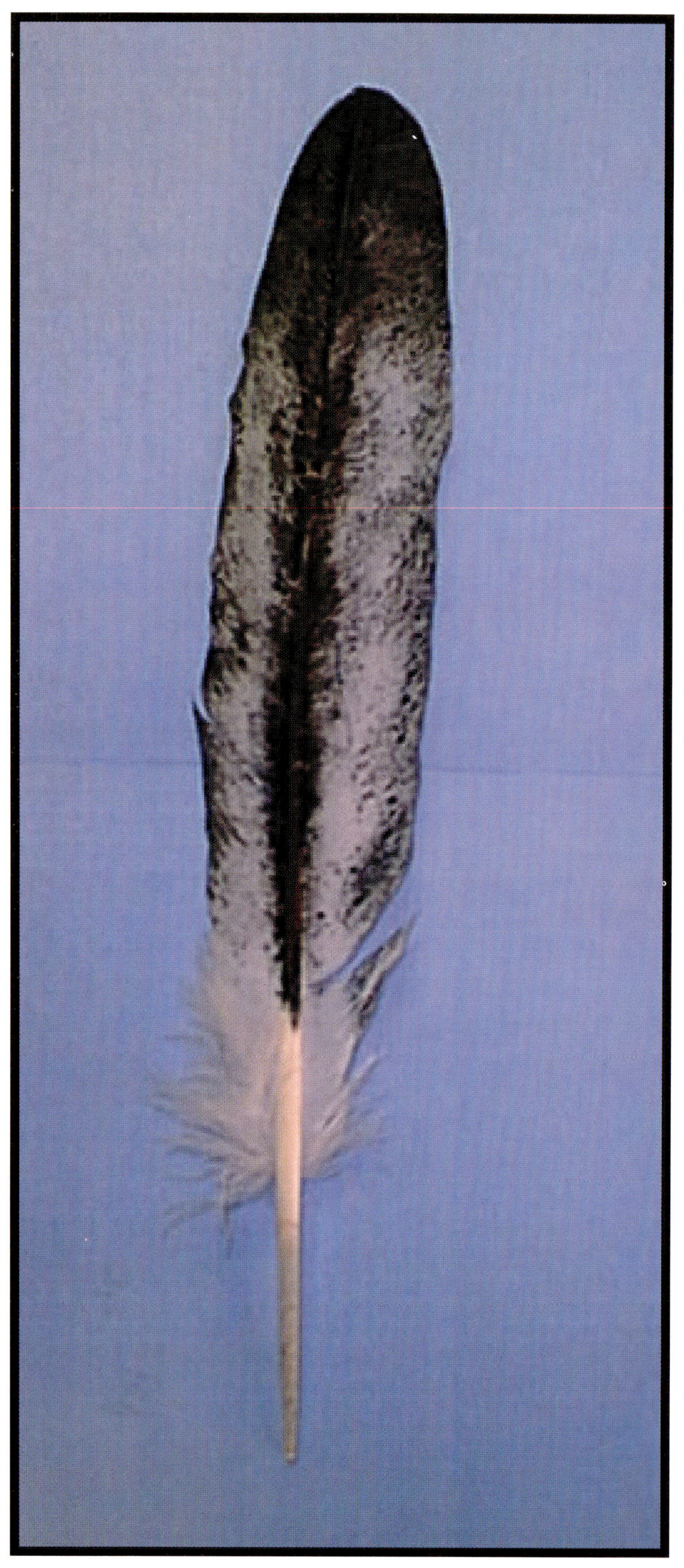

Even if the feather is totally dark representing a very immature bird the design must still be created using a stipple.

Regardless of the species or phase of bird being represented the trimming and finishing of the feather is the same as described earlier in this book.

Feathers of any predatory bird species can be simulated using the basic techniques described in this book. As long as the designs are based on sound observation of actual feathers or good photographs the results should be satisfying.

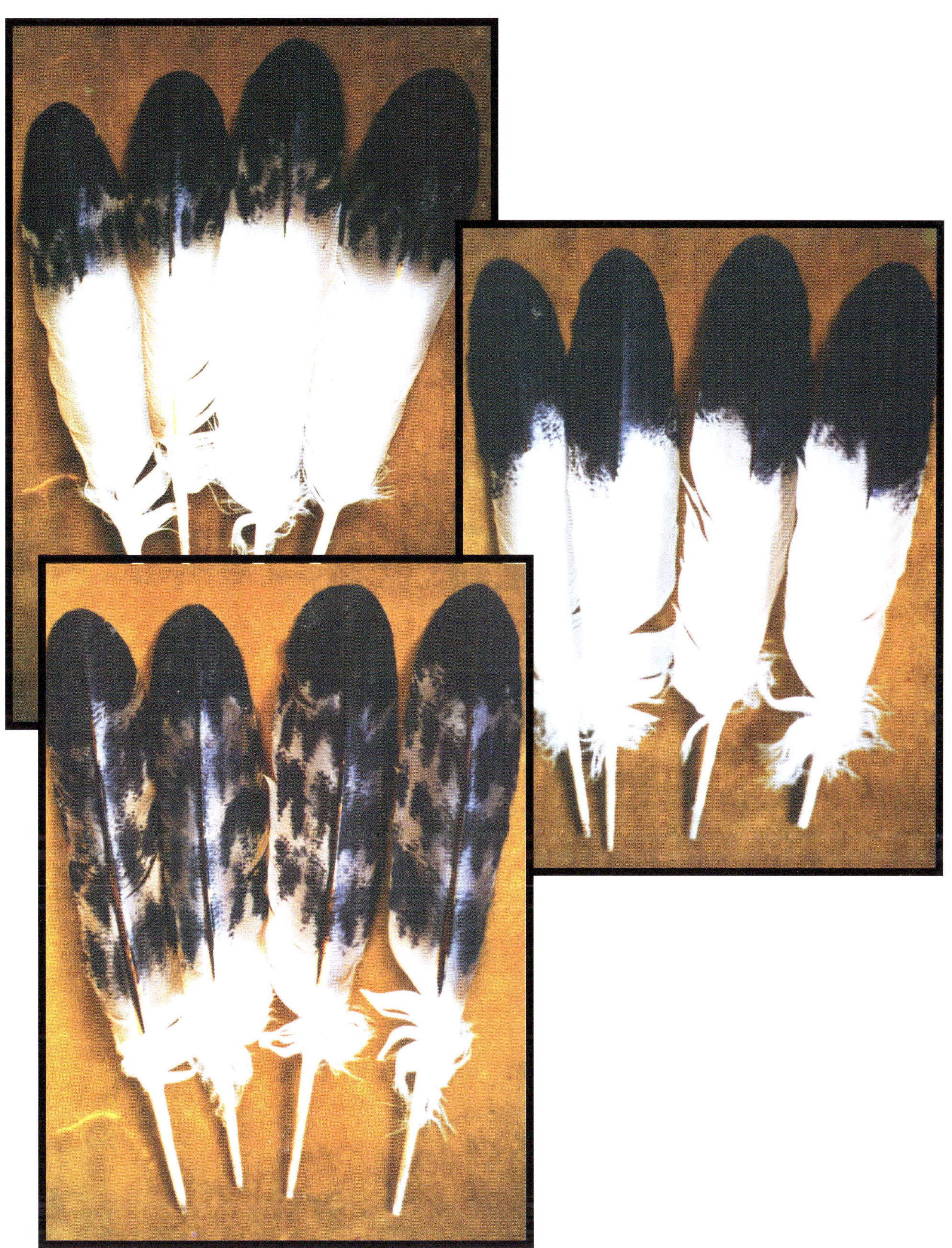

Here are some examples of feathers created using the techniques described in this book.

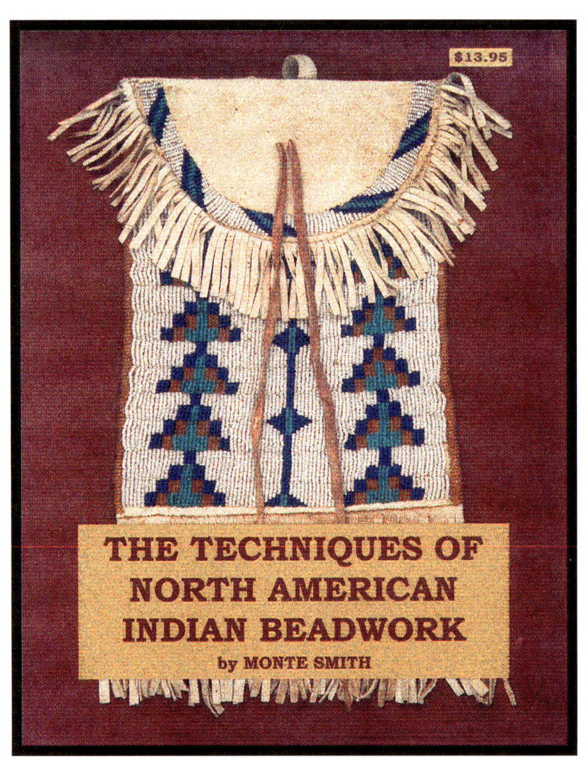

THE TECHNIQUE OF NORTH AMERICAN INDIAN BEADWORK
By
MONTE SMITH

This informative and easy to read book was written by noted author and editor Monte Smith and contains complete instructions on every facet of doing beadwork. Included is information on selecting beads; materials used (and how to use them); designs, with a special emphasis on tribal differences; step-by-step instructions on how to make a loom, doing loom work and the variations of loom work; applique stitches including the lazy stitch, "crow" stitch, running stitch, spot stitch and return stitch; bead wrapping and peyote stitch; how to make rosettes; making beaded necklaces; and, a special section on beadwork edging. There is also a section of notes, a selected bibliography and an index.

The book features examples and photos of beadwork from 1835 to the present time from twenty-three Tribes.

Anyone interested in the craft work of the North American Indian will profit from owning this book.

B00/02 - $13.95

HEMP MASTERS:
Ancient Hippie Secrets for Knotting Hip Hemp Jewelry
By
MAX LUNGER

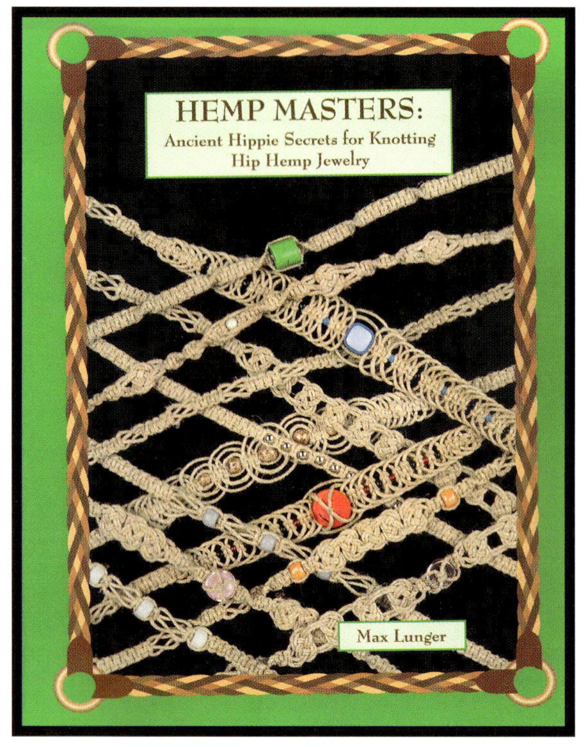

Learn to create with hemp. With the basic techniques taught in this book you can make Bracelets, Anklets, Necklaces, Chokers, Car Mirror Charms, Key Chains, Wall Tapestries, Plant Hangars, Speaker Hangers, Hackysacks and much more. Hemp jewelry making is the latest craze and it is easy to learn. After introducing the subject matter and terms used, the various knots needed are explained and fully illustrated. Included are details on incorporating beads within the knotting. After explaining how to begin a piece and providing useful tips on avoiding common problems, patterns for a variety of pieces are provided. This book is chock full of photographs (including a full color section) and has lots of illustrations. Written for both beginning and seasoned crafters, this volume should prove invaluable for any person wishing to learn more about hemp knotting - Don't miss out on this exciting new craft technique.

B00/31 - $13.95

TRADITIONAL INDIAN BEAD & LEATHER CRAFTS

By

MONTE SMITH & MICHELE VanSICKLE

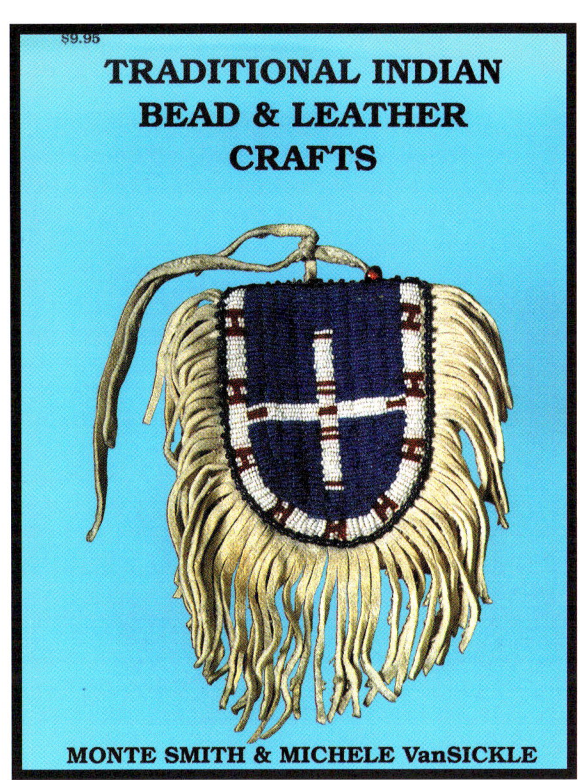

Projects described and explained include the leather pouch, strike-a-lite pouch, knife sheath, beaded Sioux pouch, scissors pouch, beaded Crow pouch, fringed pouch with rosette, beaded awl case, quilled pipe bag, fringed mirror pouch, fringed possibles pouch and gage d'more pouch.

In addition, craft techniques described include all of the basics of working with leather, lazy stitch, running stitch, "crow" stitch, spot stitch, return stitch and porcupine quill wrap.

The book is designed so that the craftsperson can choose to make any one of the illustrated projects without having to read the whole book; or, it will serve as a "primer" on the basics of traditional beadwork and leather crafts of Native Americans for the person who wants to understand these techniques and, thereby, be able to construct other items.

B00/11 - $9.95

VOICES OF NATIVE AMERICA:

Native American Instruments and Music

By

DOUGLAS SPOTTED EAGLE.

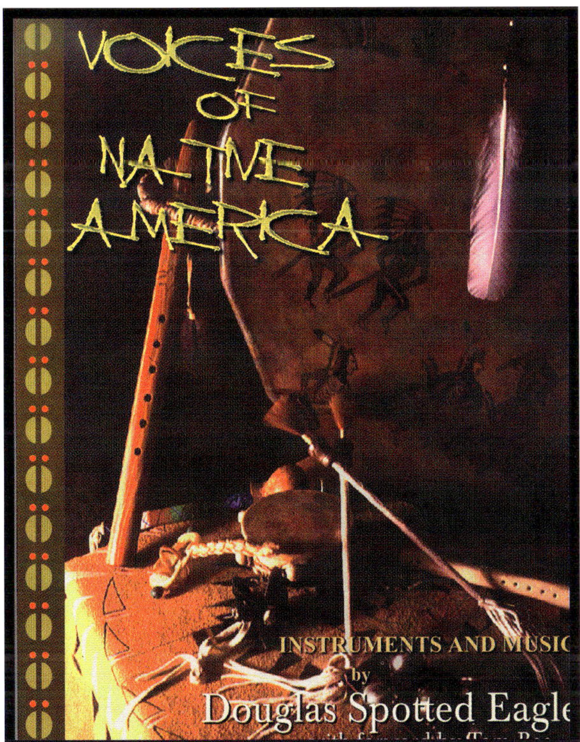

Douglas Spotted Eagle, celebrated flutist and recording artist, performs his Native American music around the world. His book not only provides a much needed discussion of the instruments and musical forms, it also gives the reader a sense of the emotion, complexity and beauty of Native American music from the perspective of a musician. The book is lavishly illustrated and contains many wonderful photographs of Native American musicians and instruments. After providing an overview of Native American music today, Spotted Eagle discusses Flutes, Drums, Rattles, Gourds, Shakers, Whistles, Rasps, Bullroarers, Snapsticks, and Fiddles. Each chapter describes the various types of each instrument and how they are made and used. The flute chapter contains a section on playing techniques. A must for anyone interested in music or Native American arts and culture.

B00/29 - $17.95

SOME EAGLE'S VIEW BESTSELLERS THAT MAY BE OF INTEREST:

	Title	Code	Price
❑	**Eagle's View Publishing Catalog of Books**	B00/00	$3.00
❑	**The Technique of Porcupine Quill Decoration**/Orchard	B00/01	$9.95
❑	**The Technique of North American Indian Beadwork**/Smith	B00/02	$13.95
❑	**Techniques of Beading Earrings** by Deon DeLange	B00/03	$9.95
❑	**More Techniques of Beading Earrings** by Deon DeLange	B00/04	$9.95
❑	**America's *First* First World War: The French & Indian War** by Todish	B00/05	$10.95
❑	**Crow Indian Beadwork**/Wildschut and Ewers	B00/06	$10.95
❑	**New Adventures in Beading Earrings** by Laura Reid	B00/07	$9.95
❑	**North American Indian Burial Customs** by Dr. H. C. Yarrow	B00/09	$9.95
❑	**Traditional Indian Crafts** by Monte Smith	B00/10	$9.95
❑	**Traditional Indian Bead & Leather Crafts** by Smith & VanSickle	B00/11	$9.95
❑	**Indian Clothing of the Great Lakes: 1740-1840**/Hartman	B00/12	$13.95
❑	**Shinin' Trails: A Possibles Bag of Fur Trade Trivia** by Legg	B00/13	$8.95
❑	**Adventures in Creating Earrings** by Laura Reid	B00/14	$9.95
❑	**Circle of Power** by William Higbie	B00/15	$8.95
❑	**Etienne Provost: Man of the Mountains** by Jack Tykal	B00/16	$9.95
❑	**A Quillwork Companion** by Jean Heinbuch	B00/17	$12.95
❑	**Making Indian Bows & Arrows...The Old Way** by Doug Spotted Eagle	B00/18	$12.95
❑	**Making Arrows...The Old Way** by Doug Spotted Eagle	B00/19	$4.50
❑	**Hair of the Bear: Campfire Yarns & Stories** by Eric Bye	B00/20	$9.95
❑	**How To Tan Skins The Indian Way** by Evard Gibby	B00/21	$4.50
❑	**A Beadwork Companion** by Jean Heinbuch	B00/22	$12.95
❑	**Beads and Cabochons** by Patricia Lyman	B00/23	$10.95
❑	**Earring Designs by Sig: Book I** by Sigrid Wynne-Evans	B00/24	$10.95
❑	**Creative Crafts by Marj** by Marj Schneider	B00/25	$9.95
❑	**How To Bead Earrings** by Lori Berry	B00/26	$10.95
❑	**Delightful Beaded Earring Designs** by Jan Radford	B00/27	$9.95
❑	**Earring Designs by Sig: Book II** by Sigrid Wynne-Evans	B00/28	$10.95
❑	**Voices of Native America: Music/Instruments** by Doug Spotted Eagle	B00/29	$17.95
❑	**Craft Cord Corral** by Janice S. Ackerman	B00/30	$8.95
❑	**Hemp Masters: Hip Hemp Jewelry** by Max Lunger	B00/31	$13.95
❑	**Classic Earring Designs** by Nola May	B00/32	$9.95
❑	**How To Make Primitive Pottery** by Evard Gibby	B00/33	$8.95
❑	**Plains Indian & Mountain Man Arts and Crafts** by C. Overstreet	B00/34	$13.95
❑	**Beaded Images: Intricate Beaded Jewelry** by Barbara Elbe	B00/35	$9.95
❑	**Earring Designs by Sig-Book III: Celebrations** by Sigrid Wynne-Evans	B00/36	$10.95
❑	**Techniques of Fashion Earrings** by Deon DeLange	B00/37	$9.95
❑	**Beaded Images II: Intricate Beaded Jewelry** by Barbara Elbe	B00/38	$9.95
❑	**Picture Beaded Earrings for Beginners** by Starr Steil	B00/39	$9.95
❑	**Plains Indian & Mountain Man Arts and Crafts II** by C. Overstreet	B00/40	$12.95
❑	**Simple Lace and Other Beaded Jewelry Patterns** by Mary Ellen Harte	B00/41	$6.95
❑	**Beaded Treasure Purses** by Deon DeLange	B00/42	$10.95

EAGLE'S VIEW PUBLISHING READERS SERVICE, DEPT EF

6756 North Fork Road - Liberty, Utah 84310

Please send me the above title(s). I am enclosing $__________ (Please add $5.50 per order to cover shipping and handling.) Send check or money order - no cash or C.O.D.s.

Ms./Mrs./Mr. ______________________________

Address ______________________________

City/State/Zip Code ______________________________

Prices and availability subject to change without notice. Allow 2 to 4 weeks for delivery.